A BEGINNER'S GUIDE TO ZEN AND THE ART OF
WINDSURFING

A BEGINNER'S GUIDE TO ZEN AND THE ART OF
WINDSURFING

A COMPLETE MANUAL OF BOARDSAILING
FOURTH EDITION—REVISED AND UPDATED

**WRITTEN & ILLUSTRATED BY FRANK FOX
WITH TECHNICAL ASSISTANCE FROM
CATHERINE BETTS & BARD CHRISMAN**

THANKS:

Thanks to my brother Paul who has spent long hours with me learning how to windsurf and encouraging me in the writing of this book. Thanks to Eva and Toni for their encouragement and hours of invaluable assistance. And thanks to Steve, Jim, Stephanie, Patrick, Brian, Debbie, Sicila, Barry, Kelly, Chuck, Bill, Richard and all those other wonderful folks who have made my windsurfing weekends so much fun.

Library of Congress Catalog
Card No. 88-070029

First Edition, August 1985
Second Edition, November 1985
Third Edition, June 1986
Fourth Edition, June 1988

ISBN: 0-934965-04-8

AMBERCO PRESS
2324 Prince Street
Berkeley, CA, 94705
10 9 8 7 6 5 4 3 2

SPECIAL THANKS:

To Lynn for her meticulous proofreading, excellent suggestions and generally being great. And to Cat for her support, enthusiasm, suggestions and criticisms.

MORE SPECIAL THANKS:

To Bill Hansen, head designer for Windwing Designs, Berkeley, CA., for his invaluable comments on sail design and performance. And to Bard Chrisman for his help on the technical issues of board repair and maintenance and sailboard performance characteristics. And to "Sei" Seiler, for his advice and consultation in the technical areas of publishing and copy preparation.

DEDICATED TO:

All those intrepid souls, male and female, young and old, who have braved icy waters, strong winds and the frustration of those first few hours of learning to make windsurfing one of the fastest growing sports today. May you always have clear skies, white sands and steady breezes.

TABLE OF CONTENTS:

NOTES ON THE FOURTH EDITION:

Well, yet another edition rolls off the presses! This one's bigger (that's good), more up to date (that's good) but, alas, more expensive (that's not so good) than the previous editions. Many thanks to all you readers that have taken the time to write with your thoughts on how the book could be improved. To the extent possible, I've included your ideas in this edition.

Many of the changes in this edition reflect the incredible advances that have been made in windsurfing technology recently. In only a few short years the sport has exploded with new applications of space-age materials, new and better methods of construction and the application of aerodynamics and hydrodynamics to design. Indeed, a modern wave board only faintly resembles a board of yesteryear.

All of this is great indeed, as long as we don't let it overwhelm us. Windsurfing is a simple sport that can be enjoyed by almost anyone. Sure, you can have the latest board and the jazziest sail, but for starters you don't need it. Just a basic board, wind and water, and you're virtually guaranteed hours and hours of fun, fun, fun. Good sailing!

F. Fox   June, 1988

PREFACE: USING THIS BOOK:

If you have no background in sailing or windsurfing, you ought to read this book in the order that I've written it. This is because there are terms that I use in the later sections which I explain in the earlier sections. Also, the maneuvers are presented in the order that they would be easiest and most beneficial to learn. The material that I felt was non-essential to the initial learning process, I included in the appendices.

But, in case you choose to skip through the book rather than read it in sequential order, I've included a basic dictionary of terms so you can look up anything that stumps you. But please don't forgo reading the sections on theory in your haste to skip to the mechanics of the maneuvers. A basic theoretical background will really help you learn your maneuvers. And whatever you do, make sure to read the first chapter! It's short and will give you a feel for my approach to the subject as well as a few hints that could help to explain things later.

When you're reading the procedures on the different maneuvers, work hard at visualizing the whole maneuver as you are reading. If there's a part of the text you don't understand, go ahead and try the maneuver on the sailboard and then read the text again. Some of the stuff is just plain hard to describe, but once you try it, it should become apparent.

And one last thought: Remember to approach this book, the sport of windsurfing and life in general with a sense of humor. After all, we're in this to have fun! And what fun it can be!!

F. Fox,   September, 1985

> HI THERE! MY NAME IS ZACHARY DOOLITTLE – A FICTIONAL CHARACTER WHOSE ROLE IT IS TO INTRODUCE YOU TO THE WET AND WILD WORLD OF WINDSURFING. SO LETS GET STARTED!!

A SHORT (AND IMAGINATIVE) HISTORY OF WINDSURFING: In the beginning there was wind. And soon thereafter humankind made sailboats. The first sailboats were surely heavy, technologically primitive and not very fast. Over the ages, however, as nautical design and construction practices advanced, sailboats got lighter, more complicated, more expensive but (unfortunately) not a lot faster. Finally, with the application of space-age technology and computer design, sailboats have reached a pinnacle of success: they've become tremendously sophisticated, outrageously complicated, prohibitively expensive but (unfortunately) not much faster.

Luckily, someone came along and bucked this rather distainful trend toward ever more complicated and expensive sailboats. They did it by inventing the "free-sail system"—what has become known generically as the "windsurfer" or "sailboard." Exactly who invented the free-sail system is open to discussion. Right now two Southern Californians named Hoyle Schweitzer and Jim Drake are being credited with inventing it in 1969. However, some people believe that the free-sail system was actually invented much earlier (figs. 1 and 2).

This new system had some major advantages over old-style sailboats. First it was much simpler than other sailboats. This meant it was easier to set up, break down and maintain than other sailboats. And this meant more time out on the water having fun and less time fooling with the boat. The simplicity of the new system also meant it was much cheaper to build and therefore buy than other sailboats. But perhaps the best feature of this new system was how fast it was! We're talking blazing speed here. I mean fast!!! No more fifteen thousand dollar boats that would top out at six knots. Now we're talking about twelve hundred dollar boats that will do twenty-five! Blistering, sizzling speed and fun to match!

TYPES OF MODERN BOARDS: Despite disagreement over exactly when the sport was invented, hardly anyone can disagree that the past five years have seen major advances in the boardsailing industry. New materials and design theories are contributing to produce a plethora of new and specialized board types: there are speed boards, slalom boards, wave boards, long boards, short boards, bobbers, sinkers and floaters. There are flat boards, round boards, fun boards and course boards. There are boards for different wind speeds or wave conditions. Boards, boards, boards!!*

What do all these different board types mean to the beginning windsurfer? Well, it's important to know there are different types of boards built to excel in different conditions. The type of board that's good for learning isn't necessarily going to be the greatest board for all the conditions you'll ever sail in. One day you will almost surely find yourself in a situation where you're having an incredibly difficult time controlling your board while everyone around you seems to be whizzing by effortlessly. Don't be too quick to blame the situation on your lack of ability! The problem could largely be due to the type of board you are sailing.

When learning, you will almost certainly be using a beginner-style board known as a "flat board." This is because this type of board tends to be stable and easy to sail in light winds. Perfect for a beginner!

However, as the wind speed increases, and with it the speed of the board, this type of board grows unstable, sluggish

FIG 1: C. 3000 BC; TIP-VORTEX THEORY AND ITS RELATION TO THE UPWIND ABILITY OF THE FREE-SAIL CRAFT AS IT WAS FIRST DISCUSSED

FIG 2: C. 1969; TIP-VORTEX THEORY AS IT WAS REDISCOVERED IN FROG CITY, TEXAS EARLIER THIS CENTURY

and difficult to control and (kersplash!) you spend a lot of time swimming. When this happens, it's time to graduate to a more advanced board, one which is designed for the higher wind conditions. Typically, you'll want to try an "intermediate funboard" or a "transition board."

Rent a more advanced board for the afternoon and see what difference it makes. You might find it makes all the difference in the world.

See Appendix One for a detailed discussion of board types.

WHAT TO EXPECT:

You might just find that windsurfing is one of the most enjoyable things you've ever tried. However, it's not without its trials and tribulations, especially during the first few months of learning. There will be times when you'll be incredibly frustrated and feel like heaving your board off the nearest bridge. But don't feel alone. Virtually everyone faces the same problems at first and, given a little tenacity coupled with an informed and thoughtful approach, you should breeze by them with relative ease. Just so you know what to expect, there are a few things we can say about learning to windsurf in general.

The first thing to realize is that sailing conditions are rarely if ever ideal. No matter! Get out there and sail! Practicing in less-than-perfect conditions is better than not practicing at all and waiting for perfect conditions will probably mean never getting to sail.

Secondly, resign yourself to the fact that you're going to spend a lot of time falling in the water and practicing your charming colloquial English. That's part of learning this sport! You're gonna feel like a klutz sometimes so get used to it. But it'll be worth it!

And finally, you should know that the maneuvers that you did perfectly yesterday when no one was watching will be

FIG 3: TECHNIQUE VISUALIZATION

impossible today in front of your friends and relatives. Small differences in conditions make a big difference in your ability to do certain maneuvers. Even world-class sailors look clumsy if the conditions are bad enough. Don't get frustrated! Or if you do get frustrated, don't give up! It'll all come to you eventually.

ZEN AND THE ART OF WINDSURFING:

The whole point of learning the rudiments of any discipline is that they become second nature and you become free to really hone and polish your natural abilities. The same is true with windsurfing. Learning the basics isn't an end. It's a beginning. And only after you know the basics can you really begin to explore the beauty and excitement of the sport.

So, the whole object in the beginning is to learn the basic techniques quickly while having as much fun as possible. To do this, you should arm yourself with some basic knowledge about the sport and the maueuvers you'll be attempting before you go out on the water. You should know the basic steps required for the maneuvers you want to perform as well as the theory behind the maneuvers. And, just as important, you should know the theory and practice behind what can go wrong. Later in the book, when you're reading through how to perform a maneuver, try to visualize the technique. Close your eyes and imagine yourself on a sailboard! Imagine the wind in your hair! Go ahead and step through the required motions, visualizing the entire process. This will make it much easier when you get out on the water although, admittedly, it might cause a few raised eyebrows if practiced in public (fig. 3).

FIG 4: THE PRACTICAL USE OF ZEN IN WINDSURFING

And above all, have patience. Many of the maneuvers just take time and practice and you'll feel clumsy and foolish at first. But frustration and a short temper won't hasten the learning process. Patience! You'll get there!!

FIG. 5: A TYPICAL NON-ZEN APPROACH

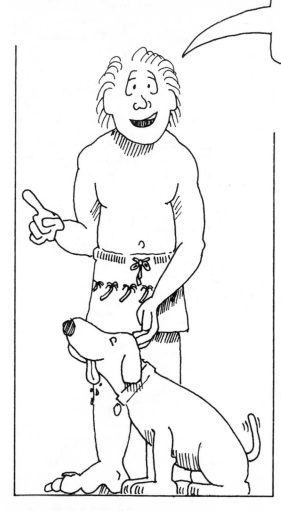

NOW, I'M SURE YOU WANT TO JUMP RIGHT ON A BOARD AND START SAILING. SORRY! FIRST WE NEED TO HAVE A SHORT DISCUSSION ON WINDSURFING LINGO & THEORY

PART ONE: WINDSURFING LINGO

Like most sports, windsurfing has its own special lingo. Some of it is borrowed from sailing, some of it is borrowed from surfing and some of it is peculiar to windsurfing.

Many beginners dread the prospect of learning all those new words. Why, they ponder, can't we just speak in plain English? Well, we could, except that we would expend an awful lot of energy on long, descriptive phrases where one or two specialized words might express the same thought. Thus, in the interest of economy, specialized vocabularies arise.

So, as dull as it might seem, you should probably try to learn some of the basic terms. Besides allowing you to give precise and accurate accounts of what you did over the weekend to your friends and co-workers, this will give you a basis of communication with other more experienced windsurfers from whom you can learn. In the following pages the terms marked with an asterisk (*) are the most fundamental and ought to be understood. Reviewing them really isn't necessary since once you start windsurfing you'll be hearing them all the time.

One final note on windsurfing lingo, especially that borrowed from the sport of sailing, is that there are often two or three names or phrases which describe the same thing. Don't let this confuse you! If someone uses a word you don't understand just ask them what it means. Chances are you're familiar with the principle but not the particular term.

WINDWARD* AND LEEWARD*:

Since the wind is an integral ingredient in windsurfing, one of the first things to learn is how to describe your board and things around it in relation to the direction of the oncoming wind.

Okay, let's visualize! Imagine yourself standing in the street in front of your house or apartment. Imagine you are standing on a sailboard. Imagine there is wind. Now point to the direction of the oncoming wind. This direction is referred to as "to windward*" (fig. 6). This means that the house you're pointing at is "to windward" of you and your imagined sailboard. Now point down by bending your hand at the wrist. You're now pointing at the windward side of your sailboard. Simple, huh?

Now turn 180 degrees and point in the opposite direction. You are now pointing "to leeward*." The bush you're pointing at is "to leeward" of you and your imagined sailboard. Pointing down at the wrist would establish the leeward side of your board.

A special note is required for the word "leeward" because it isn't pronounced the way it's spelled. In order to say the word properly you must imagine your mouth full of marbles. Then add a little mumble. It should come out something like "l'eurd" or "l'rd." This is kind of like an Army drill sergeant yelling "F'RD LEF HARSH!!" when he really means "forward left march." Who knows whence such strange customs come?

POINTS OF SAIL:

In addition to being able to describe the position of your board in relation to things around it, you'll also want to know how to describe the direction of your board's movement in relation to the angle of the oncoming wind. This is important because the technique you use to sail the board depends on the board's relationship to the direction of the wind.

There are three basic "points of sail" or relationships your board can have with the wind. First there is "pointing*." This is when you sail with the front of the board as far to windward as possible (fig. 7). Being "strapped" or "on the wind" or "going upwind*" or "going uphill" or "close-hauled" or "beating" all mean the same thing as pointing.

"Running*" refers to sailing along with the wind so that the front of the board is pointed to leeward. This is also called "going downwind*" or "downhill."

Anything between pointing and running is called "reaching*." There are different degrees of reaching. When you're almost pointing but not quite, you refer to it as "close reaching." Sailing a course perpendicular to the wind is called

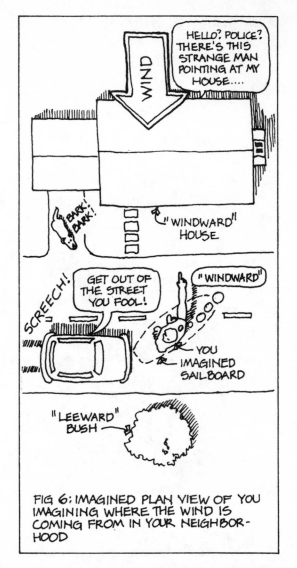

FIG 6: IMAGINED PLAN VIEW OF YOU IMAGINING WHERE THE WIND IS COMING FROM IN YOUR NEIGHBORHOOD

"beam reaching." And anything between beam reaching and running is called "broad reaching." Both reaching and running are sometimes referred to as sailing "off the wind."

In actuality, when you're first learning to windsurf, you won't be doing much pointing or running. Reaching is the most fun and the first thing you learn. Pointing you do when you want to get to windward for some reason (e.g., you're racing). Running is difficult on beginner type boards and next to impossible on shorter, more advanced boards, except, of course, for "running into the dock," which is a different sense of the word, point of sail independent, and done by almost everyone.

There is also special lingo to describe changing course from from one point of sail to another. Going from off the wind to on the wind is referred to as "heading up." When you do this inadvertently, forced by the pressure of the wind on the sail, it is called "rounding up*."

The opposite—going from on the wind to off the wind—is called "bearing away" or "falling off." The latter of these two terms, of course, can have other implications when you're learning to boardsail.

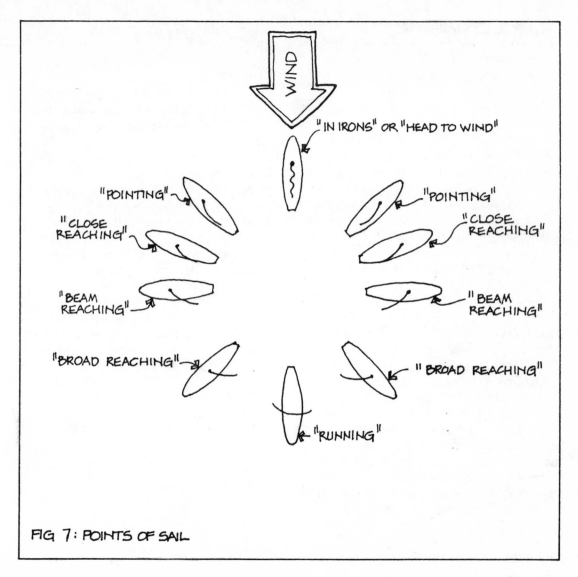

FIG 7: POINTS OF SAIL

PORT* AND STARBOARD*:

Of course, we don't only talk of sailboards in their relation to the wind. We also refer to them independently of the wind. And usually we use special terms for this.

For instance, the front of the board is called the nose* or bow, while the back of the board is called the tail* or stern. The right-hand side is called starboard* while the left-hand side is called port*.

Then, to confuse you even further, the great inventors of sailing lingo combine the terms which refer to the board with terms which refer to the wind. Two very important examples of this are the terms "starboard tack*" and "port tack*." Starboard tack refers to any point of sail where the windward side of the board is the starboard side. Port tack refers to any point of sail where the windward side of the board is the port side. Now look back at figure 7. Which side of the diagram represents the starboard tack? The left side! That's because on those points of sail the windward side of the board, the side closest to the direction of the oncoming wind, is the starboard, or right-hand, side of the board. Confused? Okay, right is starboard and left is port. In the diagram, on the left, the wind is coming over the right side of the board. On the right it's coming over the left side of the board. So if starboard is right, left is right and right is wrong!

Right? Right! Good! On to something else!

TURNING:

We also combine terms which refer to the board with terms which refer to the wind when we describe how a board turns. There are two ways a board can turn. One is called "tacking*." This is when a board turns such that its nose passes through the direction of the oncoming wind (fig. 8) and is generally what you do if you are sailing upwind. Don't confuse "tacking" with being "on a tack" (either port or starboard) which is always the case unless you are in the process of turning.

The other method of turning is referred to as "jibing*." This is when you turn the board such that its tail passes through the direction of the oncoming wind (fig. 9) and is generally what you do if you are sailing downwind. Don't confuse "jibing" with "jiving" which windsurfers tend to do even more than jibing.

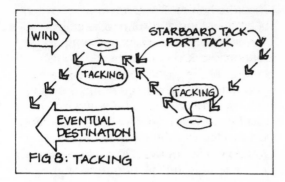
FIG 8: TACKING

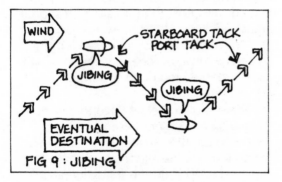
FIG 9: JIBING

FIG 10: JIVING

DESCRIBING THE WIND:

We also use words which describe the wind itself. There are four such words you ought to know: lift*, header*, gust and lull. The first two refer to a change in wind direction. The second two refer to a change in wind speed.

To "get a lift" or "be lifted" means that the wind direction changes so that you can point more in the direction you want to go (fig. 11). A header is just the opposite—a change in wind direction so that you now point less in the direction you want to go (fig. 12).

Gusts are sudden increases in wind speed. Lulls are sudden decreases in wind speed. The practical ramifications of lifts, headers, gusts and lulls will be discussed in the following chapters.

An additional note is that nautical wind speeds are usually measured using nautical miles per hour, or "knots*" (an abbreviation that defies all but phonetic logic). A knot is just a little more than a mile per hour. For example thirty knots is equal to about thirty-five miles per hour.

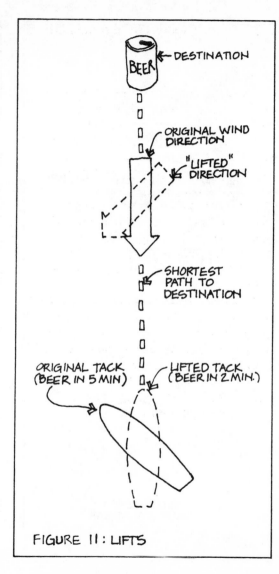

FIGURE 11: LIFTS

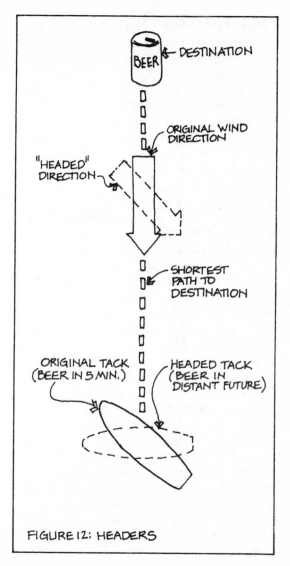

FIGURE 12: HEADERS

RIGHTS OF WAY:

Before you get out on the water, you'll want to know the lingo and rules which govern who has the right of way when two boats meet. The most important rule is the "don't get in a wreck at all costs" rule. This is self-explanatory. Another important rule is the "tonnage rule." This rule states that anything bigger than you has right of way over you. When you're on a sailboard, this refers to almost anything that floats.

   If you're ever in a situation where these two rules don't provide satisfactory answers, there are others that can be consulted. When two sailboats meet three rules apply. First, a starboard tack has right of way over port tack (fig. 13). Second, a leeward boat has right of way over a windward boat (fig. 14). And third, an overtaking boat must stay clear of the boat being overtaken (fig. 15). Always remember that not everyone knows or understands these rules.

   When windsurfers meet, common courtesy dictates that the more experienced sailor should maneuver around the less experienced sailor. In any case, you should always make your intentions clear before the situation becomes critical. This means don't come roaring up on starboard tack, pointing to windward of a port tacker, and suddenly bear off at the last second to go to leeward of

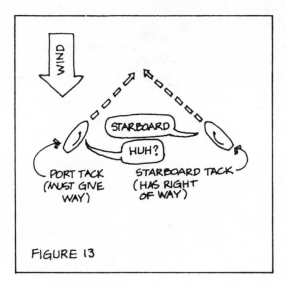

FIGURE 13

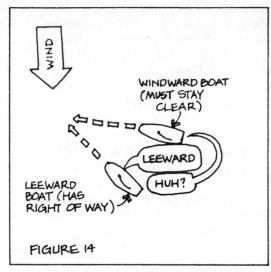

FIGURE 14

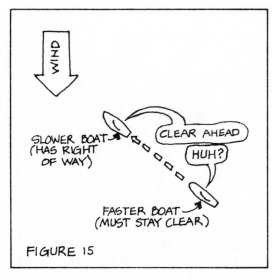

FIGURE 15

Zen and the Art of Windsurfing

him. Even though you have the right of way, you must give him or her ample opportunity to avoid a collision.

When sailboats and powerboats meet, the powerboat must generally give way. This is not always the case!!! A notable exception is when a sailboat meets a large powerboat in waters of restricted maneuverability, i.e.—anywhere but in the open ocean. If this is the case, the more maneuverable boat must give way. And if you're on a sailboard, that's you! If you are in doubt as to the size classification of the powerboat you meet or the restricted maneuverability of the waters you're in, go ahead and give it the right of way. Coast Guard investigations and lawsuits against major shipping firms are very hard on bereaved relatives.

In fact, it's good practice to avoid other boats altogether whenever possible. Never press your right of way just to prove a point. Be especially wary of freighters and other large commercial ships. They travel deceptively fast, cannot abruptly stop or turn to avoid you and block a lot of wind. Careful!!!

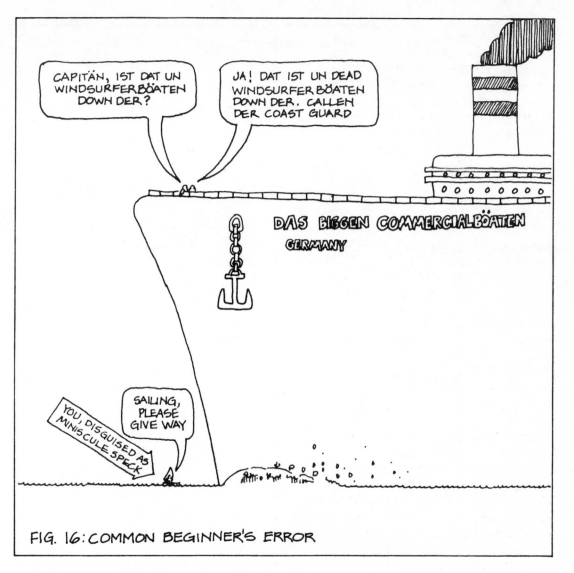

FIG. 16: COMMON BEGINNER'S ERROR

PARTS OF THE SAILBOARD:

In order for you to understand the rest of this book as well as the boardsailing magazines and talk by other windsurfers, you'll have to familiarize yourself with some of the different parts of the sailboard and what they do. Memorizing them is not necessary but you might have to refer back to these pictures in the chapters that follow. Again, the most important terms are marked with an asterisk (*).

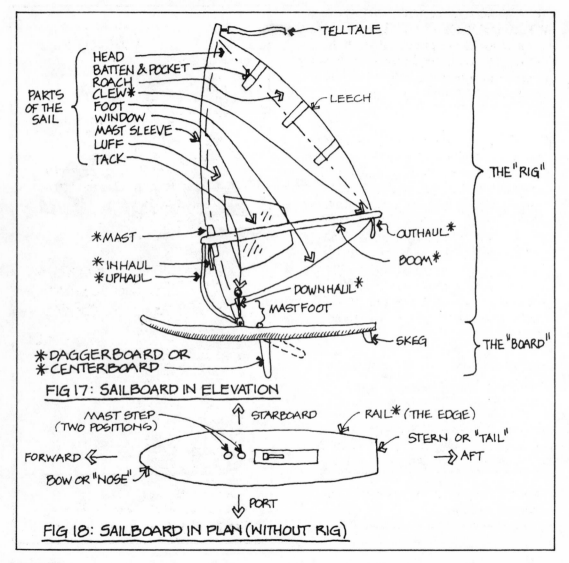

TELLTALE

PARTS OF THE SAIL

HEAD
BATTEN & POCKET
ROACH
CLEW*
FOOT
WINDOW
MAST SLEEVE
LUFF
TACK

LEECH

THE "RIG"

*MAST
*INHAUL
*UPHAUL

OUTHAUL*
BOOM*
DOWNHAUL*
MASTFOOT

SKEG

THE "BOARD"

*DAGGERBOARD OR
*CENTERBOARD

FIG 17: SAILBOARD IN ELEVATION

MAST STEP
(TWO POSITIONS)

↑ STARBOARD

RAIL* (THE EDGE)

STERN OR "TAIL"

FORWARD ←←

→→ AFT

BOW OR "NOSE"

↓ PORT

FIG 18: SAILBOARD IN PLAN (WITHOUT RIG)

IN THE ORDER OF THE COSMOS, MY CHILDREN, SUCH MATERIAL POSSESSIONS HAVE LITTLE SIGNIFICANCE.

YES, BABA UPHAUL

FIG 19: SAILBOARD IN PERSPECTIVE

Zen and the Art of Windsurfing

WHAT SOME OF THE PARTS DO:

Inhaul*: Attaches the mast to the boom.

Uphaul*: What you use to pull the sail up out of the water.

Outhaul*: Attaches the clew of the sail to the boom. Used to stretch or "tune" the sail.

Downhaul*: Attaches the tack of the sail to the mast. Also used to tune the sail.

Daggerboard* and Skeg*: Provide lateral resistance (see section on theory).

Centerboard*: Like a daggerboard but it can be pivoted back and retracted into the board.

Special Note: The distinction between a daggerboard and a centerboard is not widely known or understood. Many times a centerboard is referred to as a "retractable daggerboard." In this book we'll make the distinction except in the cases when we could be referring to either, in which case we'll use the term daggerboard.

WINDSURFING EQUIPMENT AND WHAT SOME OF IT DOES: If you're one of those lucky people that lives in the tropics, all you'll need besides a sailboard to go windsurfing is a bathing suit. If you're less fortunate, you'll need a wetsuit.

Wetsuit: Keeps you from freezing your fanny off. All kinds and styles are available. A two piece "long john and jacket" is versatile but the one piece is a little warmer. Wetsuits come in different thicknesses from about 1/8th inch (3 millimeter) to about 1/4 inch (5 millimeter) and the thicker the suit the warmer it is. Also there are many wetsuits on the market made especially for windsurfing. These tend to work better than those made for diving because they aren't as confining.

Harness: Relieves arm fatigue. Covered in detail in Chapter 4.

Gloves: Keep hands warm and relieve chafing. Leather sailing gloves work well for chafing. For warmth you'll want the special windsurfing gloves.

Booties: Keep your toesies warm and improve footing.

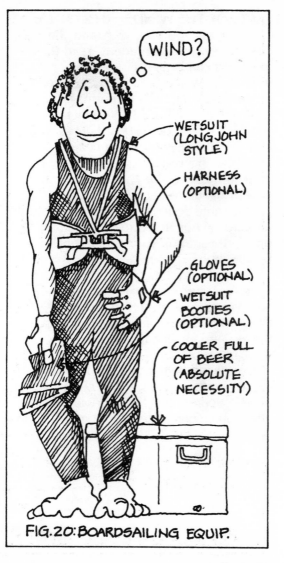

FIG. 20: BOARDSAILING EQUIP.

PARTS OF THE WINDSURFER (YOU):

In order for you to understand the descriptions of the maneuvers in the following chapters, it's important for you to know how we describe our different appendages (fig. 21). In normal sailing position, we call our hand which is nearest the nose of the board our "forward hand*." Likewise, our hand nearest the tail is the "back hand*." Some people refer to these as the "mast hand" and "boom hand" respectively. Your feet get the same designation. The one furthest forward is your "forward foot" and the one furthest aft is your "back foot." Simple, huh?

Well, it gets a little more complex. When you turn the board, you'll reverse your position on it. In the middle of the turn it becomes fuzzy as to which is the forward appendage and which is the back appendage. For this reason we'll also apply the terms "old" and "new" to the appendages. Hence the "old back hand" becomes the "new forward hand" after you've completed the turn.

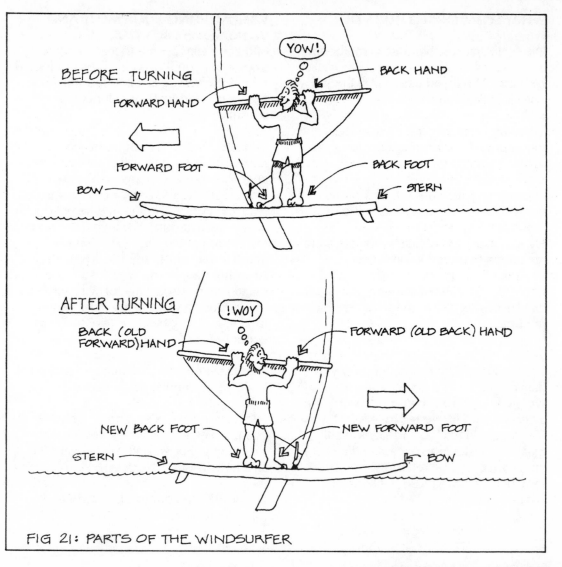

FIG 21: PARTS OF THE WINDSURFER

CHAPTER TWO: PART TWO: WINDSURFING THEORY:

Theory, it turns out, is a hard subject to broach. After all, why can't we just deal with facts? They did come first! Theory just tries to explain them!

Well, theory does have its place. It helps you analyze what's happening when things aren't going quite right. For instance, suppose you've just fallen off your sailboard for the seventh time in a row. It helps to rest a couple of minutes and think the whole thing through before you just repeat the same mistake again.

Theory, of course, has its limitations. At best, the theorists can only present us with a simplified model or idea of what's actually going on. As it turns out, the interaction of the wind, the water and the sailboard is a very complex thing and we don't fully understand it. But, through observation, it has been possible to extract some general rules and governing principles.

THE THEORY OF STEERING:

Much of the relevant theory about sailboarding revolves around how you steer. If you come to the sport from another type of sailing, one of the first things you'll notice about sailboards is the apparent lack of any apparatus which might enable you to steer the thing. This is kind of like getting into your new car and finding out there's no steering wheel.

But not to worry! Sailboards can be steered! It's done by moving the rig in relation to the board. With a little practice, you can go pretty much anywhere you want to go.

In nautical lingo and theory, when you move the rig in relation to the board, you are moving the "center of effort" (CE) of the sail in relation to the "center of lateral resistance" (CLR) of the board. Let's take these one at a time.

The CE could be defined as the imaginary focal point of all the aerodynamic forces acting on the sail. This is easier to understand with an example. Suppose you held up a square piece of cardboard exactly perpendicular to an oncoming wind (fig. 23). The CE of the cardboard would be at its exact center. The same sort of focal point is established when a sail fills with wind but it is not usually at the exact center of the sail.

The CLR could be defined as the imaginary focal point of the resistance of the board to moving sideways through the water. This resistance is established by a combination of the daggerboard, the skeg and the friction between the underside of the board and the water.

You can think of the CE and the CLR as two force vectors which work to counteract one another. By manipulating their

FIG 22: ALTERNATIVE TO CE STEERING

FIG 23: CE OF IMAGINARY CARDBOARD

relationship, you can steer the board. Clear as mud, huh?

Okay, let's try an example. Suppose you were in waist-deep water standing next to your board (fig. 24). Now put your finger on the edge of the board and attempt to push it sideways through the water. If the board pivots as you push, adjust your finger position so that you can push it exactly sideways without it turning. Once you've done that you've found the CLR of the board.

Now imagine a friend in the water with you but on the opposite side of the board. You be the CLR and imagine your friend pushing with equal force on the other side of the board simulating the CE. As long as you and your friend are pushing exactly opposite one another, the board won't turn (fig. 25). But if your friend moves forward on the edge of the board and pushes what happens? The board begins to turn (fig. 26)! The same is true when your friend moves aft and pushes (fig. 27). Yow! The theory of steering a sailboard!

But, as all you budding physicists out there already know, it's not quite that simple. How does a sailboard manage to move forward through the water if the forces acting upon it only act in a direction perpendicular to it, thereby forcing it sideways through the water? Well, to explain the theory of steering, it's easiest

FIG 24: FINDING THE CLR

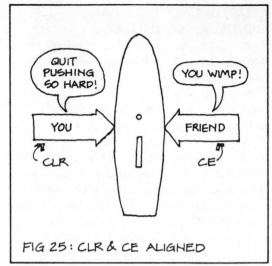

FIG 25: CLR & CE ALIGNED

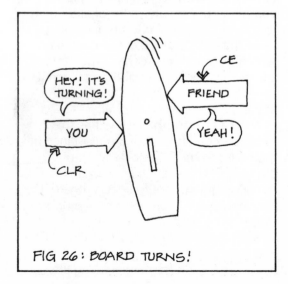

FIG 26: BOARD TURNS!

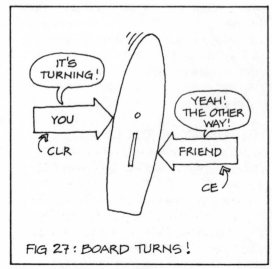

FIG 27: BOARD TURNS!

to only look at the component vectors acting in this direction. Obviously you want the sail to generate a force that pulls the board forward and this does indeed happen.

If you add the forward force generated by the sail to the CE and the resistive force generated by drag to the CLR, you end up with a CE and CLR that are aimed a little forward and aft respectively (fig. 28). The same principles govern steering, however! The sailboard will only go in a straight line if the CE and CLR are aligned. By moving the CE in relation to the CLR you can make the board turn! You do this by pivoting the whole rig forward and aft, side to side, or some combination thereof, depending on your point of sail.

When you are pointing or close reaching, this movement is forward and aft. In order to steer more to windward, you rake the whole rig aft (fig. 29). This moves the CE aft of the CLR and pushes the nose to windward. In order to steer more to leeward, you rake the rig forward. This pushes the CE forward of the CLR and pushes the tail to leeward (fig 30).

When you are running or broad reaching, the steering principle of offsetting the CE and the CLR is still the same but you have to move the rig across the

FIG 29: COMING UP

FIG 30: FALLING OFF

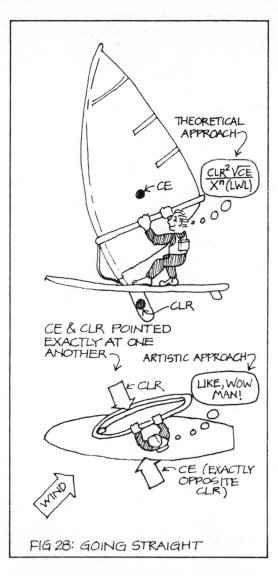

THEORETICAL APPROACH

$$\frac{CLR^2 \sqrt{CE}}{X^n (LWL)}$$

CE

CLR

CE & CLR POINTED EXACTLY AT ONE ANOTHER

ARTISTIC APPROACH

LIKE, WOW MAN!

CLR

CE (EXACTLY OPPOSITE CLR)

WIND

FIG 28: GOING STRAIGHT

board to get the offset (figs. 31 and 32).

Those of you who have sailed before and all you fast learners will realize that as the turn in figure 32 progresses you will soon be sailing with the clew of the sail toward the nose of the board. This is referred to as "sailing by the lee" and is usually done just prior to jibing. The ramifications of this will be covered in the next chapter.

FIG. 31: COMING UP (WHEN RUNNING)

FIG. 32: FALLING OFF (WHEN RUNNING)

SAIL AND WIND INTERACTION:

Now that you understand some of the basic theory behind steering, we can address the somewhat finer points of sails and sail trim.

Sails interact with the wind in two basic ways. When you are pointing, the sail acts like an airfoil by establishing a low-pressure area to leeward which acts to pull the sail and board along (fig. 33). To maximize the efficiency of the low-pressure area, the air flow must be smooth along both sides of the sail.

The other way in which a sail will interact with the wind is by simply being pushed by the wind (fig. 34). This is what happens when you are broad reaching or running. You are still establishing a low-pressure area to leeward but this effect does not require smooth air flow on both sides of the sail.

Both these effects act on the sail when you are beam reaching (fig. 35). For this reason on many boats a beam reach is its fastest point of sail. This is certainly true with sailboards!

Depending on how the sail is interacting with the wind, the center of effort (CE) of the sail will be located at different points of the sail. If the CE shifts locations while you are sailing, the sail can become difficult to handle. Generally speaking, the CE will shift for one of two reasons. First it's possible that a sail will actually change shape during a gust or lull. This changing of shape, caused either by stretching the sail cloth or bending the mast, will cause the CE to shift.

The CE can also shift due to a shifting area of "flow separation." Flow separation is simply the point on the leeward side of the sail at which smooth air flow becomes turbulent. If the area of flow separation moves forward, so does the CE.

An unstable CE can cause you to do some spectacular, although undesired, things (see pg. 73). In high and gusty wind conditions, your ability to control the CE of the sail is largely dependent on the design and age of the sail. Poorly designed and old, baggy sails can be really hard to handle. For more on this, see pg. 126, MASTS BOOMS AND SAILS.

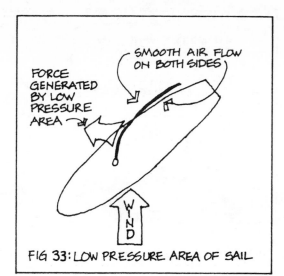

FIG 33: LOW PRESSURE AREA OF SAIL

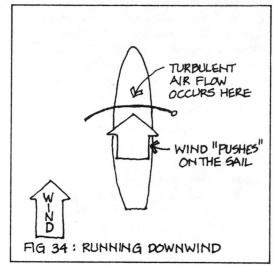

FIG 34 : RUNNING DOWNWIND

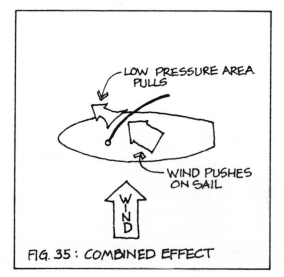

FIG. 35 : COMBINED EFFECT

FIG 36: LOW PRESSURE AREA OF BERKELEY

APPARENT WIND:

The last area of theory every budding sailor should know about is something called "apparent wind." This subject typically causes much confusion but when understood, it can do much to explain the interaction between the sailboard and the wind.

"Apparent wind" is exactly what the term implies. It is where the wind appears to be coming from and and how hard it appears to be blowing. This will differ from the "true wind"—the actual speed and direction of the wind taken at a stationary observation point—if you are moving at all.

Okay, suppose on a windless day you were driving your convertible at forty miles per hour (fig. 37). The velocity of the car through the stagnant air mass would create an "induced wind" of forty miles per hour coming from your direction of travel. That is, if you were to stand up on your seat you would feel a 40 MPH wind hitting you in the face. In this case, your apparent wind (40 MPH) would equal your induced wind (40 MPH).

But suppose you were driving at forty miles per hour and that there was also a true wind coming from your right at forty miles per hour (fig. 38). You wouldn't feel two separate winds, but instead one "apparent wind" which

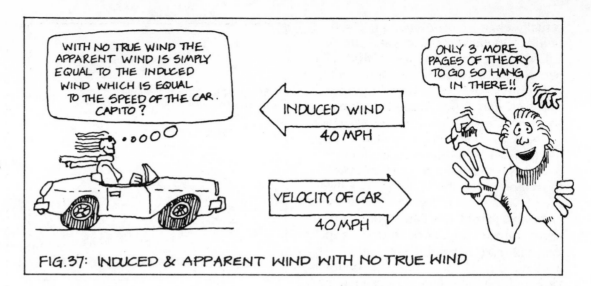

FIG. 37: INDUCED & APPARENT WIND WITH NO TRUE WIND

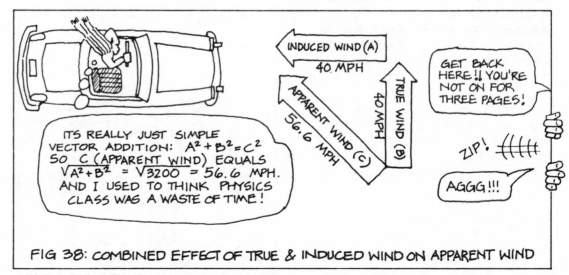

FIG 38: COMBINED EFFECT OF TRUE & INDUCED WIND ON APPARENT WIND

resulted from the combined effects of both the induced and true wind.

Of course, on your sailboard you won't ever have any induced wind if there is no true wind, unless you bolt on an outboard motor! The important thing to realize is that the direction and speed of the wind when you are sailing is not the same as when you are stationary.

Since the apparent wind results from the addition of the true and induced winds, when the true wind increases or decreases there is a shift in both the apparent wind speed and apparent wind direction.

In the case of a gust, your apparent wind will not only increase but it will also shift in direction to windward (fig. 39). As a result, you will have to trim the sail for your new point of sail even though your direction hasn't changed. If you were pointing as high as possible, a gust will allow you to be lifted.

The effect during a lull is just the opposite. Your apparent wind speed decreases and your apparent wind direction shifts to leeward (fig. 40). The effect is the same as getting a header.

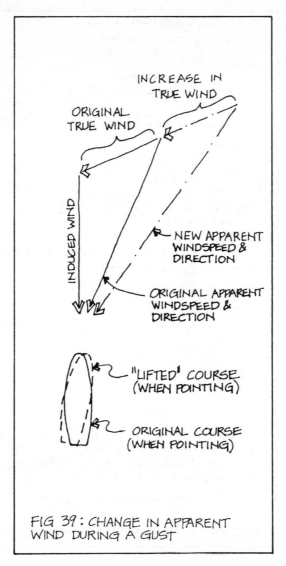

FIG 39 : CHANGE IN APPARENT WIND DURING A GUST

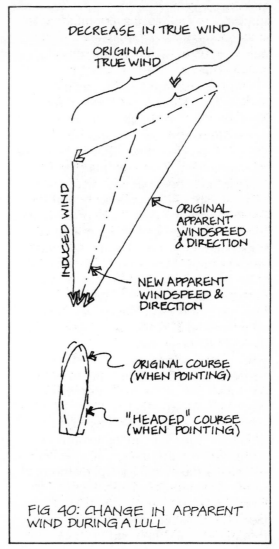

FIG 40: CHANGE IN APPARENT WIND DURING A LULL

SAIL TRIM:

Trimming sails just refers to pulling them in or letting them out. Pulling them in is called "sheeting in." Letting them out is called "sheeting out."

Usually, you trim a sail in order to develop maximum power. When this is the case, you are "properly trimmed." If you are oversheeted or undersheeted, the sail won't be performing at its maximum efficiency. On a sailboard, you sheet in and sheet out with your back hand. To sheet in, you simply pull the boom toward the center line of the board. To sheet out, you ease tension with your back hand and let the boom end swing away from the center line of the board.

An undersheeted sail is easy to recognize because it will be "luffing" or flapping in the wind like a flag. The more undersheeted it is, the greater portion of the sail will be luffing.

An oversheeted sail is "stalled." This happens when you want smooth air flow on both sides of the sail in order to create an airfoil effect but the sail is sheeted in too far creating turbulent flow on the leeward side. In light winds, a stalled sail is hard to recognize because it looks very much like a properly trimmed sail. In high winds, stalling the sail can cause you to do some fairly nasty things (See: The Catapult, pg. 73). Proper sail trim comes with time and practice.

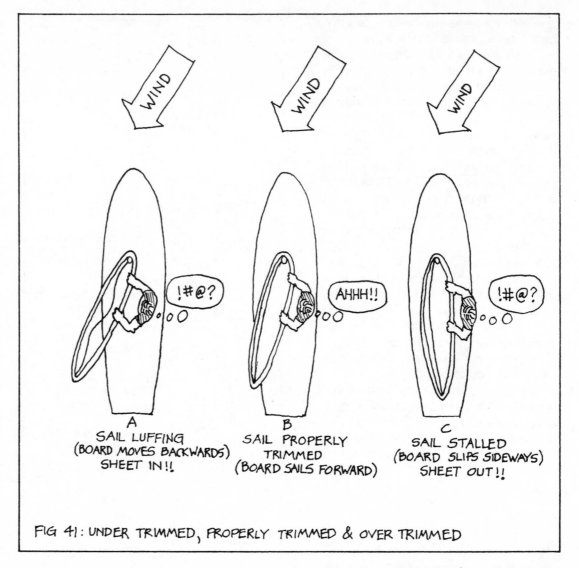

FIG 41: UNDER TRIMMED, PROPERLY TRIMMED & OVER TRIMMED

Okay! That's it! That's all the lingo and theory you need to know not only to start windsurfing but also to jive with all those neat people you'll soon be meeting.

If you want to know how much of the info you've retained, take the lingo and theory test (fig. 42). Answer all the questions by checking the appropriate box. Then score yourself and find out what category you fit into. The answers are listed (upside down) at the end of the scoring section.

And remember: when you're jiving with other more experienced windsurfers, ask questions!! Compare what they tell you with the theory you know and the experiences you've had. Talk it up! Don't be timid! Windsurfers are nice people!

WORD	ANSWER (CHOOSE ONE)						WORD	ANSWER (CHOOSE ONE)					
	SAILING TERM	CUSS WORD IN FRENCH	SOMETHING TO EAT	YOUR DOG'S NICKNAME	FAMOUS SINGER	OTHER		SAILING TERM	CUSS WORD IN FRENCH	SOMETHING TO EAT	YOUR DOG'S NICKNAME	FAMOUS SINGER	OTHER
WINDWARD							BOOM						
LEEWARD							MAST						
POINTING							BOOTIES						
REACHING							RIG						
RUNNING							FORWARD						
PORT							AFT						
STARBOARD							LUFF						
TACK							STALL						
JIBE													
LIFT													
HEADER													
BOW													
STERN													
UPHAUL													
DOWNHAUL													
INHAUL													

SCORING:

# CORRECT ANSWERS	CATEGORY
22+	PARLEZ VOUS FRANÇAIS?
19-21	A BORN SAILOR
12-18	A GOOD PROSPECT
8-11	A FAIR PROSPECT
5-7	BLAME IT ON THE BOOK
0-4	GET YOUR MONEY BACK

ANSWERS: THEY'RE ALL CUSS WORDS IN FRENCH!!

FIG. 42: SAILING LINGO & THEORY QUIZ

OKAY! ENOUGH WITH THAT BORING THEORY JAZZ! LETS START SAILING!! IN THIS CHAPTER WE'LL BE TALKING ABOUT CHOOSING A PLACE TO START AND THE FIRST COUPLE OF MANEUVERS YOU'LL BE LEARNING.

GRR...

PICKING A PLACE TO START:

The first few hours you spend learning to windsurf may be some of the most frustrating hours of your life. If you've ever watched beginners learning, you'll know why. If not, you'll soon find out!

One of the best ways to keep this frustration to a minimum is to be careful about choosing the place you'll be learning (fig. 43). Sometimes you just have to take what you can get, but if you have a choice, try to pick a spot with the following features.

Wind: Anything between four and eight knots is fine, but what you really want is steady wind. Gusty and shifty wind or extremely light wind makes learning very difficult.

Sandy Beach or Dock: Rocky shores are very hard on the board and your feet. Try to find a place with a small boat-launching dock or, even better, a nice sandy beach.

Calm Water: Big waves are for later in your illustrious career. At first, even a six inch chop will make learning a lot more difficult.

Of course, depending on exactly how you choose to learn to sail, your choice of sites might be limited. If you're the type who benefits from such things, you might choose to take a lesson. Typically this will cost between thirty and sixty dollars and take anywhere from an afternoon to an entire weekend. Or you might just rent a board and try it yourself. Rental places sometimes require that you've taken a lesson before you can rent a board, so call ahead! Boards usually rent for between eight and fifteen dollars an hour with an extra dollar or two an hour for a wetsuit. Considering you can get an adequate used beginner's board for between four and six hundred dollars, renting a lot isn't something you'll want to do.

PRECAUTIONS:

When first starting out, there are a couple things you should know to keep from doing yourself bodily harm or causing yourself embarassment and defeat. First you should know that every beginning windsurfer since the dawn of time has ended up to leeward of where he or she has started. So make sure there are no mean things to leeward of your carefully chosen starting place. Mean things include, but are not limited to, rocky shores, big ships or large expanses of open ocean.

For this reason, a spot with an onshore (blowing toward the shore) or cross-shore (blowing parallel to shore) wind is best. Offshore breezes can get you in trouble. High winds can also get you in trouble, so at first don't go out in over ten knots.

Another thing you must consider is the effect of tides and currents. Unfortunately, currents are much harder to discern than wind direction so ask someone familiar with the area if there are normally any currents which would cause you to drift to somewhere you'd rather not be.

Also, wind patterns often change predictably over the course of a day so check that out with the locals. Nothing dampens a beginning windsurfer's spirits

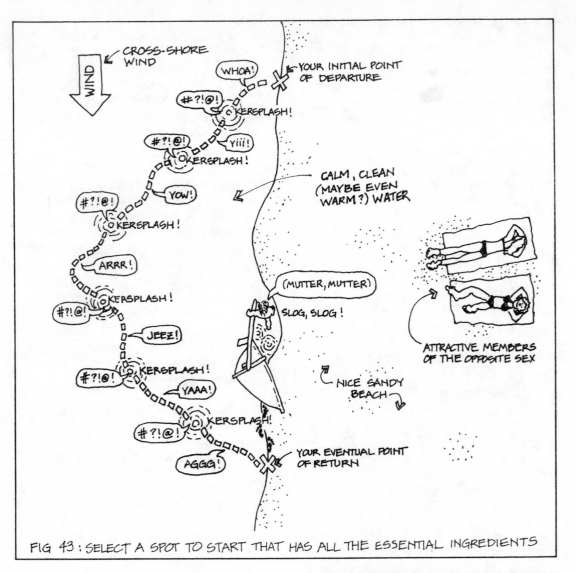

FIG 43 : SELECT A SPOT TO START THAT HAS ALL THE ESSENTIAL INGREDIENTS

like getting caught in a gale the first time out!

Before you actually venture out onto the water always be sure to make a quick check of your gear. Look for obvious signs of wear or damage. A broken mast foot half a mile from shore can ruin an otherwise perfect day.

If, once you get out on the water and despite all your best efforts, you find yourself drifting further and further from where you want to go, you might end up having to do a self rescue. This consists of rolling up your sail and lashing it, along with the boom, on top of your board. Then climb aboard and paddle back (fig. 44). Never leave the board and attempt to swim back. Distances over water can be very deceiving!!

If you find yourself unable to sail or paddle back and the conditions become extreme, you become exhausted or cold or it's getting dark, don't hesitate to ask for help. Inform nearby sailors of your plight or signal for help by waving both hands in a crossing pattern above your head. Always put your safety first and your pride second!!!

And one thing to be extremely cautious about is hypothermia. This is a lowering of body temperature caused by exposure to the cold. Hypothermia is first characterized by shivering. In the later stages, it can cause loss of motor control, uncon-

FIG 44: PADDLE BACK OR SIGNAL FOR HELP IF YOU CANNOT SAIL BACK

sciousness and, in extreme cases, death. Do not take hypothermia lightly!! If you find yourself shivering, go back to shore and warm up! Only those who have suffered from the intermediate stages of hypothermia know how quickly it can come on and how incapacitating it can be.

RIGGING THE BOARD:

If you buy or borrow a board to learn on, you'll have to rig it before you can go sailing. Almost every board rigs differently but the basic principles are the same. Once you get used to it, it will take you only five to ten minutes to rig the average board. At first, however, you ought to allow at least a half hour.

The first thing to do is to unfold the sail and slip the mast into the mast sleeve. If you have a fully battened sail, either an RAF or a camber-induced sail (see pgs. 126, 129, 145-6), you'll either have to withdraw the battens 18" or so or feed the camber inducers smoothly over the mast to enable you to insert the mast into the sleeve.

Next, attach the boom to the mast with the inhaul. Many methods exist to do this so you'll have to figure out which method your boom uses or ask someone for help. The rule is: MAKE THE INHAUL TIGHT AND MAKE SURE IT'LL STAY TIGHT!! Loose booms are a drag!!

FIG 45: PROBLEMS ASSOCIATED WITH OFFSHORE WINDS AND/OR CURRENTS

When rigging the inhaul, make sure not to position the boom too high on the mast. Try for about shoulder height. Much higher than that makes sailing difficult at first. Remember when you're positioning the boom in the mast sleeve opening that when you tighten the downhaul, it will pull the sleeve opening lower on the mast.

The next step is to rig and tighten the downhaul (fig. 47). First, if you have an adjustable mast base, adjust it so that when the downhaul is tight, the sail will be as close to the board as possible. This will take some trial-and-error efforts on your part but it's time well spent. The closer the sail is to the board, the easier it will be to control.

The tightness of the downhaul depends on the wind strength. The harder the wind is blowing, the tighter you'll want it. For starters, make it medium tight. This means pull plenty hard but don't pretend you're Godzilla. Wait until you start sailing in stronger winds. Then pretend you're Godzilla!! When you tighten the downhaul, vertical wrinkles will appear along the luff of the sail. Not to worry! We'll get rid of those in the next step.

Now rig the outhaul (fig. 48). When you do this make sure the clew of the sail is to leeward of the mast, otherwise the wind might flip the sail over while you're

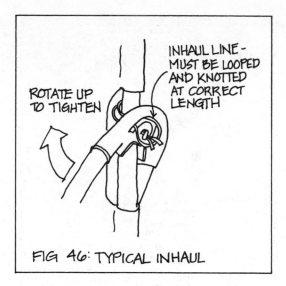

FIG 46: TYPICAL INHAUL

ROTATE UP TO TIGHTEN

INHAUL LINE - MUST BE LOOPED AND KNOTTED AT CORRECT LENGTH

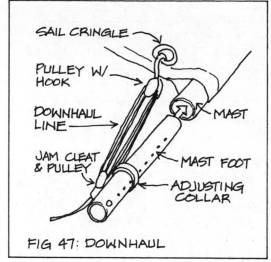

FIG 47: DOWNHAUL

SAIL CRINGLE

PULLEY W/ HOOK

DOWNHAUL LINE

JAM CLEAT & PULLEY

MAST

MAST FOOT

ADJUSTING COLLAR

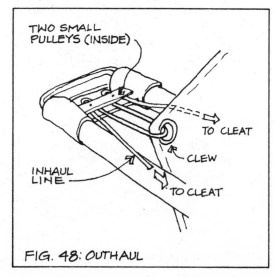

FIG. 48: OUTHAUL

TWO SMALL PULLEYS (INSIDE)

TO CLEAT

CLEW

INHAUL LINE

TO CLEAT

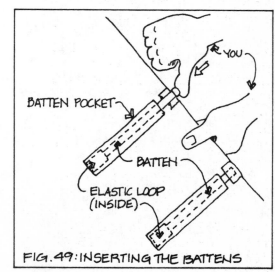

FIG. 49: INSERTING THE BATTENS

BATTEN POCKET

YOU

BATTEN

ELASTIC LOOP (INSIDE)

working. Tighten the outhaul until the vertical wrinkles disappear but not so much that horizontal wrinkles appear parallel to the foot of the sail. Again, let the wind strength be your guide. If it's blowing fairly hard, you'll want to flatten the sail by increasing the downhaul and outhaul tension. This will cause the sail to develop less power and it will be easier to control. Don't overdo it though. A completely flat sail tends to stall easily and therefore becomes hard to control. If you're sailing in light winds, you'll want to ease the outhaul and downhaul a bit to increase fullness and power in the sail.

If your sail is old, you might not be able to adjust the outhaul and downhaul so that all the wrinkles disappear. This is just because sails tend to stretch out of shape with use. Oh well, do your best!

If your sail has battens, now's the time to put them in. For non-fully-battened sails, the batten pockets are usually spring loaded with a loop of elastic which will hold the batten in a fold of cloth. Simply push the batten into the pocket past the fold of the cloth and release it so that it seats properly (fig. 49).

If your sail is a fully battened version, first get some extra tension on the outhaul. Then push the battens all the way down into the batten pockets making sure they seat properly. Next, tension the battens. Good and tight!!! Then, beat your

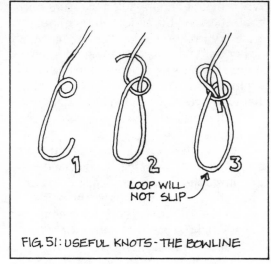

FIG. 50: ATTACHING THE MASTFOOT

FIG. 51: USEFUL KNOTS - THE BOWLINE

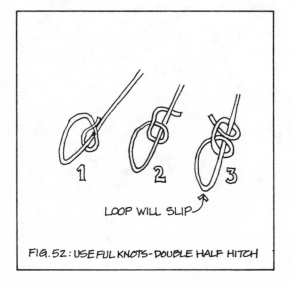

FIG. 52: USEFUL KNOTS - DOUBLE HALF HITCH

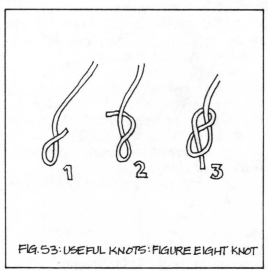

FIG. 53: USEFUL KNOTS: FIGURE EIGHT KNOT

chest a few times and do a Godzilla number on the downhaul. Fully battened sails almost always need more downhaul. And last, ease the outhaul a little to get some "camber" or fullness in the sail. Easy, huh?

Now, all that's left to do is attach the rig to the board. There are many different systems for this. They usually involve pushing a button, pulling a pin, twisting a flange or some combination thereof. So push, pull and twist until you figure it out.

When you are trying to figure out how to attach the mast foot to the board, look for any type of adjustable gizmo at the mast step. Many mast feet have a mechanism which allows the rig to separate from the board in the case of a bad fall. Sometimes, you can adjust the sensitivity of the release mechanism. Look for a knob or screw that might do this and make sure it isn't real loose, thereby allowing the mast to pop out all the time.

Finally, be sure to attach your tether line to the base of your mast. This is a small line, the other end of which attaches to the bow of the board or somewhere around the mast step. In the event of rig separation it will prevent the board from surfing or drifting off before you can get to it.

FIG. 54: MAKE SURE YOU KNOW THE EXACT WIND DIRECTION

THE WIND DIRECTION:

So now, with the board all rigged, you're ready to jump in the water and sail off into the sunset. Wait!! There are a couple more things to cover. One of them is developing a sensitivity to the wind direction.

Almost all of the maneuvers you'll be performing require a distinct relationship to the wind and if you don't have that relationship, you'll spend most of your time swimming.

Get used to establishing the exact direction of the wind prior to each maneuver you attempt. And keep paying attention to your relationship to the wind during the maneuver.

CARRYING THE RIG:

Often it is easiest to rig the sail on the beach or in the parking lot, carry the board and the rig to the water separately and then attach and tether the rig there. There are some tricks to this which could save you embarassment as well as physical injury.

The board isn't too much of a problem. You should remember, however, that it's big and can catch a lot of wind. Carrying it on top of your head in high winds can be tricky, as the wind can catch it and slam it bow or stern first into the ground.

Carrying the rig is a bit trickier. There is one rule to remember: ALWAYS HANDLE THE RIG WITH THE MAST TO WINDWARD!! In high winds, let the head of the sail trail to leeward a bit. This includes when you are carrying the rig, rigging it up, leave it laying around, putting it in and taking it out of the water and everything else: MAST TO WINDWARD!!!

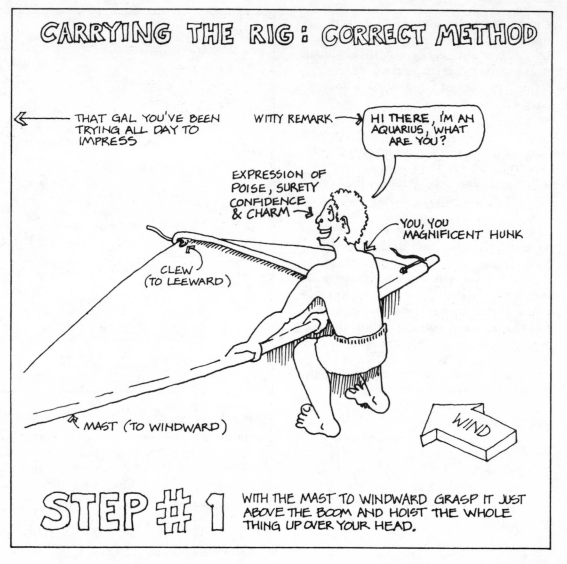

To carry the rig, just hoist it over your head so that the mast is positioned to windward. If the top of the mast feels like it wants to lift up, pivot the whole thing on the top of your head so that the head of the sail trails off to leeward a bit.

Then you just walk where you want to go! Just keep the mast positioned to windward and you shouldn't have any problems. To turn, simply pivot your body beneath the sail so that the mast is always pointed to windward, changing hand positions as necessary.

One thing that you should be aware of is that when you are carrying the rig, it acquires a special type of physio-magnetic force that attracts it to the backs of bystanders heads, cars with recent paint jobs and chain link fences. You must constantly work to counteract this force while carrying the rig.

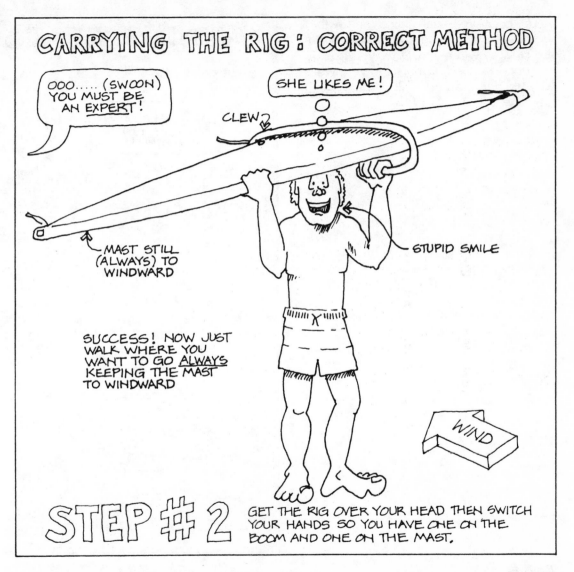

The opposite of carrying the rig with the mast to windward is carrying it with the clew to windward. After you do this once, you will understand very well why we don't sail our sailboards with the clew to windward!!

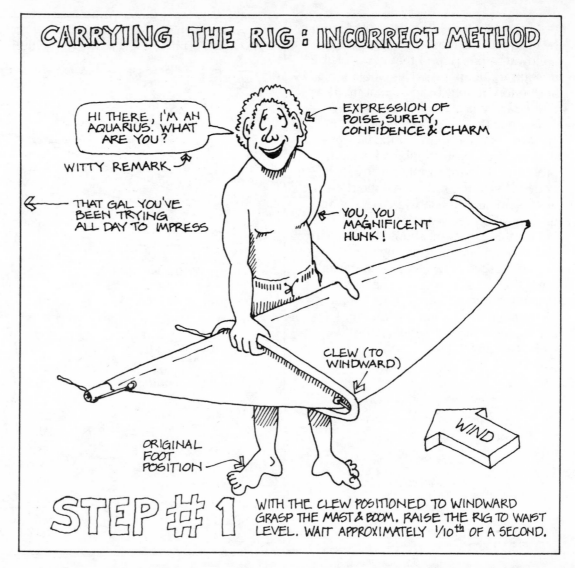

Zen and the Art of Windsurfing

If you choose not to handle the rig with the mast to windward, that's okay because the sail will tend to establish its own equilibrium with respect to its orientation to the wind. This is sometimes referred to by windsurfing plastic surgeons as the "free nose job."

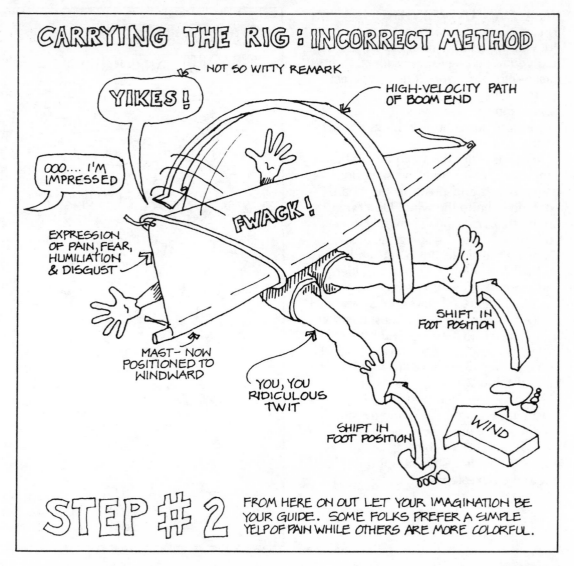

BASIC MANEUVERS:INTENDED

1) Land-Based Simulation: Okay, you've got your rig and board at the water's edge and you're itching to start sailing. Wait! First, go for a dry run. It helps you get a feel for the wind in the sail before the board is in the water where it's unstable, free to turn and a host of things can go wrong.

To make your board into a land-based simulator, just remove the skeg and daggerboard and position the board perpendicular to the wind. Don't do this on the rocks or asphalt or you'll wreck your board. Look for soft grass or sand.

Attach the rig to the board and stand on the board with your feet shoulder width apart and equally spaced around the mast step. Grab the uphaul and lift the rig until the mast almost hits you in the nose (the mast is standing approximately straight up). Then move aft until you can brace your forward foot just behind the mast. After that, grab the boom about 4 or 5 inches behind the mast with your forward hand (or simply hold the mast just below the boom if that's more comfortable). Okay, is the mast still standing straight up? It is? Good! On to the next step!

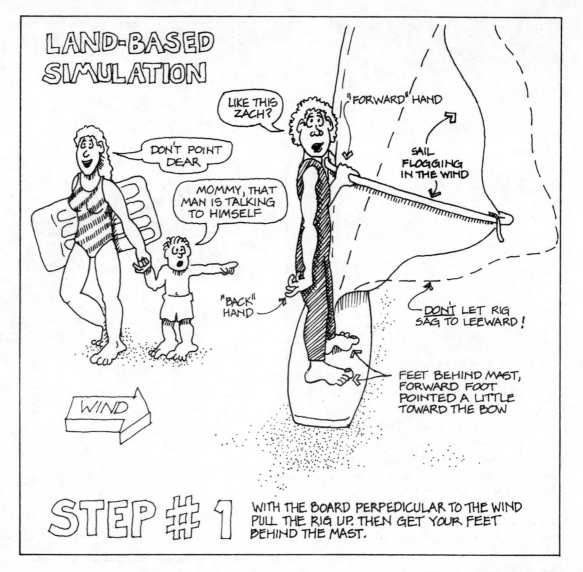

LAND-BASED SIMULATION

"LIKE THIS ZACH?"

DON'T POINT DEAR

MOMMY, THAT MAN IS TALKING TO HIMSELF

"BACK" HAND

"FORWARD" HAND

SAIL FLOGGING IN THE WIND

DON'T LET RIG SAG TO LEEWARD!

FEET BEHIND MAST, FORWARD FOOT POINTED A LITTLE TOWARD THE BOW

WIND

STEP #1

WITH THE BOARD PERPEDICULAR TO THE WIND PULL THE RIG UP. THEN GET YOUR FEET BEHIND THE MAST.

The next motion is perhaps the most important in all of beginning Windsurfingdom. It entails balancing the pull of the sail against your body weight. Ready? Okay, pull the mast JUST PAST YOUR FORWARD SHOULDER raking it FORWARD* and across the board TO WINDWARD*. Remember: FORWARD AND TO WINDWARD!! Okay? At the same time lean back, reach out with your back hand, grab the boom and sheet in. Make sure you lean back BEFORE you sheet in fully. Sheeting in and then leaning doesn't work. Have faith!! The wind will hold you up!

The whole sequence should be one flowing motion and you should end up balanced perfectly against the pull of the sail. You control the pressure of the wind in the sail by sheeting in and out with your back hand. Easing with your forward hand is a prelude to disaster. Don't do it!

If you have a hard time with this maneuver, check for three things: make sure you get the rig FORWARD AND TO WINDWARD, make sure you're leaning BEFORE you sheet in and make sure you're not easing with your forward hand when you feel overpowered.

*If you don't understand FORWARD AND TO WINDWARD, see Appendix 4, pg. 147

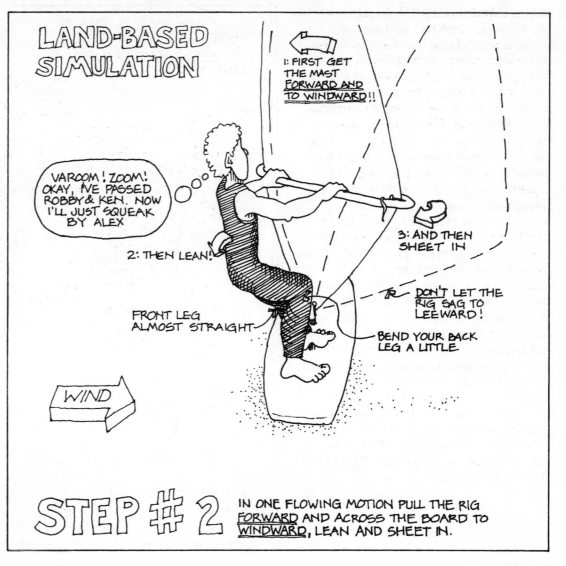

GUSTS AND LULLS:

As the wind gusts, you'll have to lean harder and as it lulls you'll have to lean less. Since the wind is almost never perfectly steady, it would be good to practice handling gusts and lulls while you're still on the land-based simulator.

During a lull, the pressure on the sail will decrease and without corrective action, you'll fall backwards into the water or, in this case, the sand. What you have to do is sheet in harder to get the sail to create maximum pressure and at the same time swing your body toward the boom to get your weight toward the center line of the board. The actual action isn't nearly as hard as sensing the lull early enough to be able to do something about it. If you're late, there's nothing really to do except going kersplash or kerplunk as the case may be. If you get tired of waiting for a lull on your land-based simulator, you can simulate one by leaning a little too far.

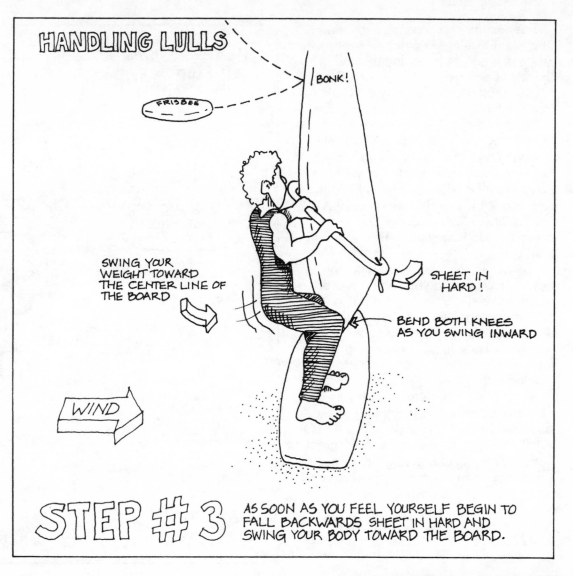

HANDLING LULLS

BONK!

FRISBEE

SWING YOUR WEIGHT TOWARD THE CENTER LINE OF THE BOARD

SHEET IN HARD!

BEND BOTH KNEES AS YOU SWING INWARD

WIND

STEP #3 AS SOON AS YOU FEEL YOURSELF BEGIN TO FALL BACKWARDS SHEET IN HARD AND SWING YOUR BODY TOWARD THE BOARD.

Zen and the Art of Windsurfing

One of the most difficult and crucial things you'll learn as a beginning windsurfer is how to handle gusts.

During a gust, the pressure on the sail will suddenly and dramatically increase. As this happens, you'll feel like you're about to be pitched across the board. To counter this tendency, you'll have to lean harder against the pull of the sail. But to do that, you must first depower the sail in order to initiate your leaning. You accomplish this by easing your back hand a little. Sometimes only a few inches will do—just enough so that you can lean further to windward. Again, never ease your forward hand or you'll be asking for real trouble.

Now, with the sail unsheeted a little, you are free to lean harder to windward and sheet in again. The whole procedure—sheet out, lean, sheet in—will become second nature after awhile. Try to get a feel for it on the land-based simulator because it's a movement you'll need to use a lot. If you get tired of waiting for gusts on your land-based simulator, try simulating some by not quite leaning far enough on your initial lean and sheet movement.

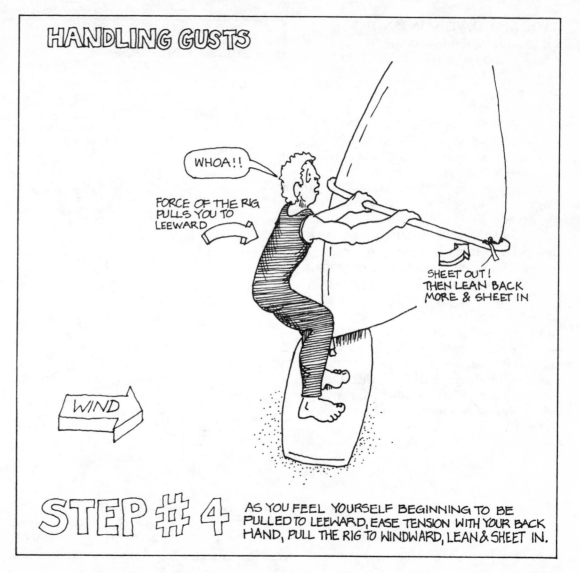

HANDLING GUSTS

WHOA!!

FORCE OF THE RIG PULLS YOU TO LEEWARD

SHEET OUT! THEN LEAN BACK MORE & SHEET IN

WIND

STEP # 4 AS YOU FEEL YOURSELF BEGINNING TO BE PULLED TO LEEWARD, EASE TENSION WITH YOUR BACK HAND, PULL THE RIG TO WINDWARD, LEAN & SHEET IN.

BASIC MANEUVERS: INTENDED

2a) Launching the Board: Okay, enough with land-based simulation. Let's start sailing!! Put the skeg back on the board, put the daggerboard in and let's get into the water!!

The process of getting your board into the water is called launching. At a beach, you usually launch the board and rig at the same time. If you're sailing from a dock, you usually carry the board and the rig down separately and attach them in the water.

Many methods of launching have been devised over the ages. Some are much less elegant than others with some tending toward the embarassing and/or physically threatening category. To keep your launches elegant and non-threatening, just remember always to handle the rig with the mast to windward. As we've seen in the section on carrying the rig, clew to windward can have disastrous consequences. Imagine what happens when you have a forty-pound board in tow!

LAUNCHING

GOLLY! THIS IS EXCITING!

WIND

DRAG THE WHOLE THING INTO KNEE-DEEP WATER

STEP # 1 — MAKING SURE NOT TO GET THE CLEW TO WINDWARD, GRAB THE BOARD WITH ONE HAND AND THE MAST WITH THE OTHER

Zen and the Art of Windsurfing

2b) Landing: The opposite of launching your board is landing it. The same basic principle applies: Mast to windward! Also, when you're sailing up to the beach, remember to pull up your daggerboard or kick up your centerboard (they're different, remember?). That will keep you from damaging it or your board should you run aground.

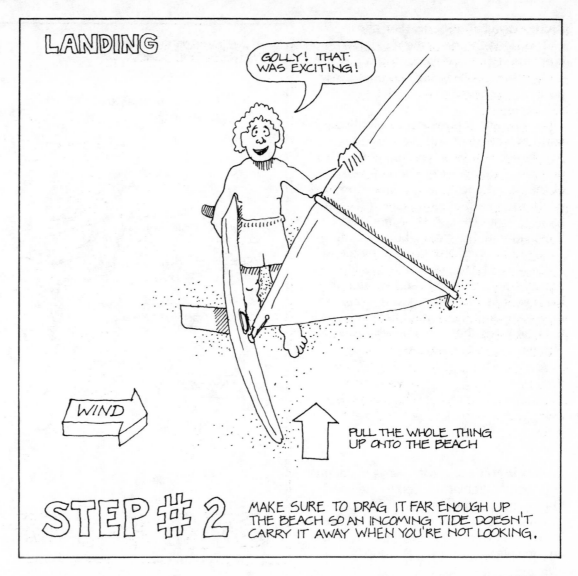

BASIC MANEUVERS: INTENDED

3) The Uphaul: This is the maneuver you'll use to get the rig up and out of the water and sail off for the first time. First, position the board in the water so that it is perpendicular to the wind with the rig to leeward and the clew pointed aft. If you have a friend with you and the water isn't too deep, you might try to persuade him or her to stand at the stern of the board and hold it in position while you climb aboard. Your end of the bargain is not to bash your friend on the head with the mast when you fall.

Friend or no friend, now's the time to climb aboard. Do everything just like you did on the land-based simulator. With your feet equally spaced around the mast step, grab the uphaul line and lean back allowing the sail to slowly come out of the water. Slow and easy!

IMPORTANT: You must always maintain your perpendicular relation to the wind during this maneuver!! Pay attention to where the wind is coming from!! See Helpful Hints (pg. 56) for hints on gaining and maintaining this relationship.

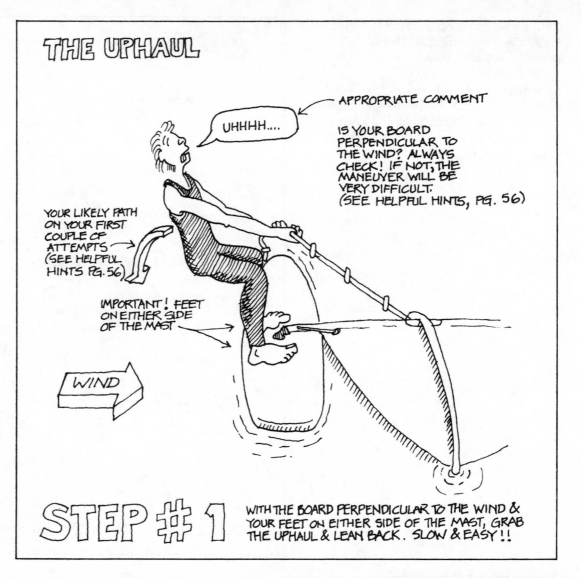

Once you get the sail up and out of the water, again check your position in relation to the wind. If you are no longer perpendicular, correct by gently pushing or pulling on the boom with your back hand. Or, you can just hold the uphaul in your hand while you rotate the board with your feet. However you do it, just make sure that the board is perpendicular to the wind before continuing. No kidding! YOU'VE GOT TO BE PERPENDICULAR TO THE WIND!! Otherwise, you'll end up a better swimmer than a boardsailor!

After you've got the board perpendicular to the wind, just hold the mast in front of you and try to relax. You'll notice that your position is a very unstable one, especially if there are some small waves. Try to gain some confidence in your balance. Hang in there!

As you gain confidence, squiggle your feet aft at least until your forward foot hits the mast. If you can, get your forward foot behind the mast like in the land-based simulation. Now check your relationship to the wind again. Board still perpendicular to the wind? Yes? Good! On to step three!

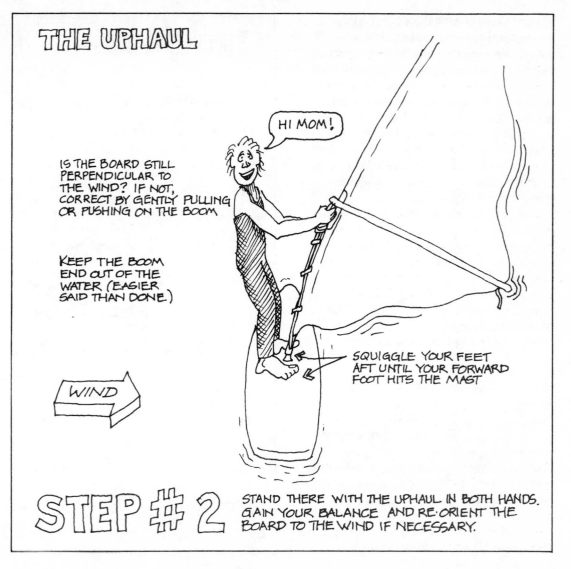

Now here comes the part you practiced in the land-based simulation. It'll be a lot harder now that you're on the water but once you get it, you're on your way.

Grab the mast just below the boom with your forward hand. (As you get better, transfer your forward hand to the boom at this point instead of holding the mast.) Then pull the rig FORWARD and across the board TO WINDWARD*. It should brush just past your forward shoulder. Then lean as you grab the boom about three feet back with your back hand and sheet in. Did it work? If not, make sure you aren't trying to sheet in with the rig held away from you at arm's length and before you lean. Make sure you're getting the rig FORWARD and across the board TO WINDWARD!! Make sure to reach at least 3 feet back on the boom before you sheet in. And make sure you're still perpendicular to the wind!!

This part of the uphaul procedure is the hardest to master. Expect to fall a lot. Practice, practice, practice!! Always check that you are PERPENDICULAR TO THE WIND, that you're getting the mast FORWARD AND TO WINDWARD and that you lean BEFORE you sheet in!!! Smile! It gets easier from here on out!

*See pg. 147 if you don't understand

Okay!! You're sailing!! Celebrate with an energetic "YAHOO!!" But don't lose your concentration or you won't be sailing for long.

Check to make sure that you're not inadvertently turning the board. Try to sail along maintaining your perpendicular relation to the wind. Try not to hit anything. If you get into trouble, your vehicle has brakes. Just drop the sail and you'll come to a roaring halt.

Once you can sail in a straight line, try turning gently to windward and to leeward. Remember that raking the rig aft will steer you up to windward and raking the rig forward will steer you down to leeward (see pp. 25-28 for review). In any case don't sail too far on one tack because you might find the opposite tack a lot more difficult so you might end up having to swim the board in.

Remember also what to do in case of lulls and gusts. For lulls, sheet in and get your body weight toward the center of the board. For gusts, sheet out a little, lean harder and then sheet back in.

As you get comfortable with your sailing, try to transfer your forward hand to the boom at this point. To do this, sheet out a little, quickly shift your hand position and then sheet back in.

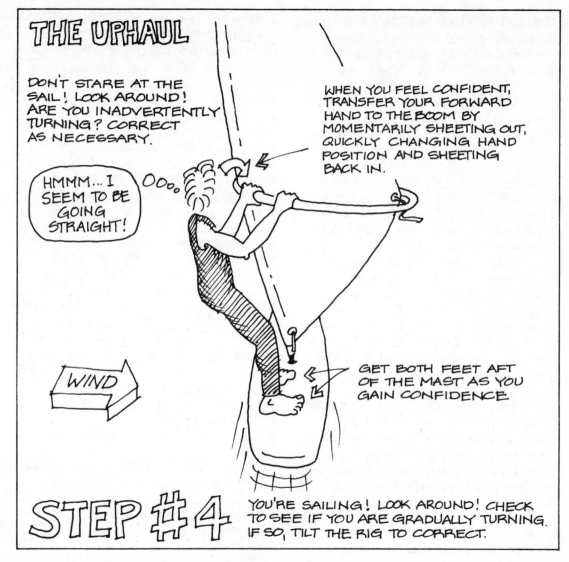

HELPFUL HINTS FOR UPHAULING:

It can take a long time to get good at uphauling. Most of all, you should know that it just takes time and practice, so don't get discouraged. But there are a few hints which might speed your progress.

One position you will find yourself in is where you fall and you pull the rig to the windward side of the board (fig. 67). Then, on your next attempt, the rig is on the wrong side of the board for uphauling. Whadda ya do? One historically proven solution is to uphaul it to windward and let it whip around to leeward. Unfortunately you don't always know which way the rig will swing, so be prepared to duck so the boom doesn't knock your teeth out.

Another way of dealing with this problem is to pull the sail partially out of the water and let it fill with wind. Provided there is adequate wind, the pressure on the sail will spin the board completely around so that the rig ends up to leeward. This also heads you in the opposite direction but, what the heck, at first the whole point is to be able to sail at all. The direction isn't all that important!! If you opt for this solution, don't expend a lot of energy trying to pull the sail fully out of the water until the rig has swung fully to leeward. Slow and easy!! Pulling really hard will just wear you out!!

Now let's ponder why this second solution works at all. What you're really doing is steering the board with the sail even though the sail is only partially out of the water! The pressure of the wind on the sail causes the board to turn completely around. You can use the same principle to maintain your perpendicular relationship to the wind as you pull the sail out of the water. If you drag the rig forward as it fills with wind, the board will steer down to leeward. If you drag the rig aft during the uphaul, the board will steer up to windward. Try it!!

This brings us to another common beginner's error. ALWAYS UPHAUL THE SAIL WITH YOUR FEET EQUALLY SPACED AROUND THE MAST STEP. Many beginners forget to do this and try to uphaul while standing with both feet aft of the mast step. If you do this, you will automatically drag the rig way aft during the uphaul which will, in turn, cause you to steer dramatically to windward and get dumped off the board. Remember: FEET EQUALLY SPACED AROUND THE MAST STEP DURING THE UPHAUL!!!

Another situation that will surely plague you is when you fall such that the rig is to leeward but the clew of the sail is pointed toward the bow of the board. To remedy this, just uphaul as you normally

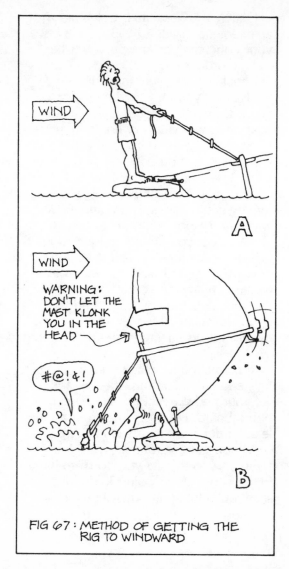

FIG 67: METHOD OF GETTING THE RIG TO WINDWARD

would. As the sail fills with wind, you'll sail backwards a little bit. But as soon as you get the boom end up and out of the water, you'll come to a stop.

Once you get the sail out of the water, there is still lots of room for error. We've already discussed the most common error but it's worth repeating. You must get the rig FORWARD AND TO WINDWARD (see pg. 147) before you sheet in! The harder it's blowing, the further to windward the mast needs to be before you sheet in. In light winds, get the mast forward and just a tad to windward as you lean and sheet in. In heavier winds, get the mast forward and further to windward as you lean and sheet in. Not doing this will cause you endless headaches.

If you don't get the rig forward as you sheet in, you'll round up and get dumped off. This is easy to recognize because the sail will fill for just a moment but then the pressure will diminish and you will get dumped to windward.

If you let the rig sag to leeward as you sheet in, you will stall the board. This is a little harder to recognize than getting rounded up. The symptoms are that the sail will be full and pulling very hard against your arms. But instead of the board moving forward through the water, it will be sort of wallowing sideways. Look at the water passing the stern of the board. If there are turbulent eddies trailing to windward, then the board is stalled.

If this is the case, chances are that your forward arm is extended allowing the rig to sag to leeward. A stall is hard to correct. You have to get the rig forward and to windward to drive the bow of the board to leeward. You'll know when you've corrected it because the board will suddenly start to move much faster and it will be much easier to sail.

BASIC MANEUVERS: INTENDED

4) The Tack: As soon as you get good at sailing in a straight line, you'll have to learn to turn around and come back. Remember from Chapter 2 that there are only two ways a sailboard can turn. It can either be tacked or it can be jibed.

The tack is the easiest to learn. It involves steering the board to windward and through the direction of the wind while stepping around the mast to the other side of the rig. During the tack, you'll be moving around on the board a lot so you'll want firm footing. If your board is slippery, wear an old pair of tennis shoes for traction. You can also buy a special type of wax that you rub on the board to give you better traction. It's available at most windsurfing and surfing shops.

To start a tack, you'll be sailing along either pointing or close reaching. To make this exciting, let's imagine that you're about to run into a large, solid, immovable object. After all, necessity is the mother of invention!!

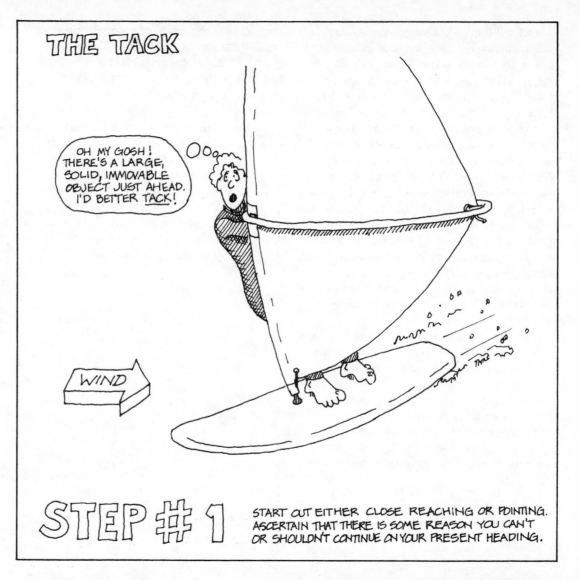

The first thing you should do to begin any turn is look aft to make sure you're not going to get into a wreck. All clear? Okay, now rake the rig way aft. Don't be timid about this. If you have a long boom, you'll probably end up dragging it in the water off the stern of the board. Don't sheet out as you rake the rig aft. It is the pressure on the sail which will push the bow of the board into the wind. The full sail also gives you something to lean against to maintain your balance.

As the board begins to turn, the pressure on the sail will decrease. When this happens, quickly transfer your forward hand to the mast.

THE TACK

RAKE RIG AFT

KEEP SAIL FULL

OKAY, NOBODY BACK THERE TO RUN INTO

TRANSFER FORWARD HAND TO MAST

WIND

STEP #2

CHECK AFT TO MAKE SURE YOU'RE NOT ABOUT TO HAVE A WRECK. ALL CLEAR? OKAY, RAKE THE RIG DRAMATICALLY AFT.

After the board has turned to windward enough that it's hard to maintain your balance, begin to walk around the front of the mast. At first in your tacking career, you'll probably be taking itty bitty little baby steps and lots of them. Later, as you become more confident, the size of your steps will increase. The really good sailors sort of hop from one side of the board to the other. Just one big step!

Even as you're stepping around the mast, keep the sail sheeted in as long as possible. This will keep the board driving through the turn and give you something to balance against.

THE TACK

RIG AFT, SAIL SHEETED IN AND FULL

LOOKS EASY, DOESN'T IT.

DRIVE THE BOARD THROUGH THE EYE OF THE WIND BEFORE YOU RELEASE YOUR BACK HAND

WIND

BOARD ALMOST STOPPED IN THE WATER

STEP # 3   KEEP THE RIG WELL AFT AND THE SAIL FULL AS YOU STEP AROUND THE MAST. THIS WILL KEEP THE BOARD DRIVING THROUGH THE TURN.

When you can no longer sheet the sail with your old back hand, release the boom and grab the mast. This hand now becomes your new forward hand on the new tack. Now the maneuver starts to look a lot like the uphaul except that the board is pointed more to windward.

Now, take a large step aft on the new side so you have a good wide stance. In the same motion, rake the rig forward with your new forward hand, reach out with your new back hand and sheet in.

Make sure to get the mast far enough forward to drive the bow to leeward. Since you'll still be pointed fairly high into the wind, you'll have a greater tendency to stall than on the normal uphaul (see Helpful Hints pg. 56). You must drive the bow down to leeward.

Some boards will have a tendency to submerge at the bow after they stall out. To counteract this tendency you have to get your weight out to the new windward rail and aft just a little bit. Then get the rig forward and sheet in to try to drive the bow up out of the water. Getting the bow of the board to come back up is hard, so don't be discouraged if you don't get it right away.

THE TACK

IMPORTANT! GET THE RIG FORWARD

SHEET IN

BOW SHOULD DRIVE TO LEEWARD

WIND

FOOT MOVES AFT

STEP #5 GET THE RIG FORWARD AND A LITTLE TO WINDWARD AND SHEET IN. THIS SHOULD DRIVE THE BOW TO LEEWARD.

After you get the board to steer down to leeward, move aft and assume a normal sailing stance. If you tacked onto a port tack, remember that you are now the "burdened tack" and you are responsible for avoiding starboard tackers.

BASIC MANEUVERS: INTENDED

5) The Jibe: You'll remember from Chapter 2 that jibing is turning the board so that the stern passes through the direction of the oncoming wind. There are many different variations on how to jibe a sailboard. The one described here is good for light to moderate winds. Jibing in higher winds requires additional techniques which we'll cover in the next chapter.

Jibing is a lot harder to learn than tacking but once learned, it's usually preferred as a more fluid and graceful way of turning a sailboard. You'll probably fall the first twenty times you try to jibe but keep at it because once you get it, boy is it fun!

To begin the jibe, you'll be sailing either on a beam or broad reach. Look back to leeward to make sure you won't get in a wreck when you turn. All clear? Okay, now reach out on the boom with your back hand to widen your grip.

To begin turning to leeward, rake the rig to windward and a little forward and sheet in with a tugging motion. Be prepared to lean harder as you do this because it will tend to yank you off balance until you get used to it. As the board turns, sheet out and keep the rig raked well to windward to keep the board turning. Remember that when you're broad reaching or running, steering is accomplished more by moving the rig across the board than by moving it forward and aft (See pg. 28 for review).

As you turn downwind, you'll notice that the wind appears to diminish. This is because you're now travelling in the same direction as the wind and your induced wind speed must be subtracted from the true wind speed in order to get your apparent wind speed. Presto! Less apparent wind!

NOTE: After you get the hang of jibing, try stepping way aft at this point in the maneuver. If you're sailing with the daggerboard fully down, also sink the (old) windward rail. This will really speed up the turn. If the board rounds up on your original tack, you've stepped back a little too early. Once the turn is complete, quickly move forward or the board will round up on the new tack.

Keep the board steering to leeward until the stern has passed through the direction of the wind and you're actually broad reaching on your new tack but with the clew of the sail aimed a little toward the bow of the board. This is called sailing "by the lee" and is a crucial ingredient to jibing in moderate winds. You'll remember, however, from the section on carrying the rig, that clew to windward is a very unstable position so you won't want to sail like this for long.

While you're steering the board onto the new course, you should switch your foot position so your stance will be proper when you jibe the rig.

THE JIBE

KEEP THAT RIG OVER TO KEEP YOU TURNING!

SO THIS IS WHAT ZACH MEANT BY "BY THE LEE."

WITH THE BOARD TURNED BENEATH YOU THE CLEW IS NOW OVER THE NEW WINDWARD SIDE. HENCE YOU ARE "BY THE LEE."

WIND

REVERSE YOUR FOOT POSITION FOR THE NEW TACK

STEP # 3

STEER THE BOARD UNTIL YOU ARE BY-THE-LEE. THEN REVERSE YOUR FOOT POSITION IN ANTICIPATION OF THE NEW TACK.

Okay, now you're all set to jibe the rig. Here is where your keen sense of timing comes into play. In light winds you'll want to drive further by the lee than in heavier winds. If, when you finally release the boom, it feels like it's getting ripped out of your hands, you've driven too far by the lee for the wind conditions. On the other hand if, when you release the boom, it's blowing off the bow of the board so that you can't reach it to sheet in, you've not sailed far enough by the lee.

Okay, so you've picked the time to jibe the rig. What now? Simply release the boom with your old back (new forward) hand. The boom will whip away from you. As it does, grab the mast just below the boom. In the same motion, step forward on the board and rake the mast FORWARD AND TO WINDWARD for the new tack.

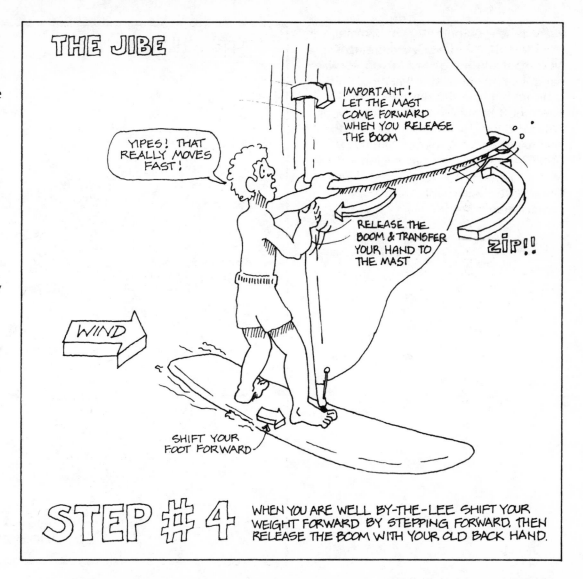

From here on out, the whole maneuver starts to look like the advanced stages of an uphaul. With the mast in your forward hand, lean to windward reach out and grab the boom with your back hand. Then sheet in and you're sailing on your new tack. Easy, huh? Just make sure to get that mast FORWARD AND TO WINDWARD before you sheet in, otherwise you'll be introduced to the "Slam Dunk" (see Basic Maneuvers: Unintended).

THE JIBE

YEAH!!!

NEW FORWARD HAND

WITH YOUR NEW FORWARD HAND ON THE MAST REACH OUT AND SHEET IT THE SAIL WITH YOUR NEW BACK HAND

WIND

STEP #5

IMPORTANT: WITH YOUR NEW FORWARD HAND GET THE MAST FORWARD AND TO WINDWARD!! THEN SHEET IN WITH YOUR NEW BACK HAND.

Once you get the board sailing on the new tack, move back on the board and transfer your forward hand to the boom. To do this, just sheet out for a second, transfer your hand and then sheet back in. Presto, you've jibed!

HELPFUL HINTS FOR JIBING:

You've heard this before but it's worth repeating. Beware of letting the rig sag to leeward! This is a real common beginning mistake on the jibe. Once you release the boom and grab the mast with your new forward hand (step #4), make sure to rake the mast FORWARD AND TO WINDWARD with a very pronounced effort. As with the uphaul, you'll have to bring the mast close to you as you move it forward and to windward. Don't hold it out there at arm's length!

BASIC MANEUVERS: UNINTENDED

Windsurfing is very easy as long as you do everything just right. If you don't do everything just right, you'll soon find that out! Two common but undesired maneuvers plague virtually every beginner. It helps to know what to expect and why so you can learn how to recognize and therefore correct the problem.

1) The Slam Dunk: This maneuver is most common when you are pointing or close reaching. It is simply an undesired and rapid turning of the board to windward. The result is a diminishing of pressure on the sail and you fall backwards. It's caused by getting the center of effort of the sail too far aft. This causes you to round up. In its milder form, it's caused by sheeting the sail in with the mast too far aft. That causes you to steer to windward. MAST FORWARD BEFORE YOU SHEET IN!

In its more dramatic form, it is caused by a gust of wind. The increased wind pressure can change the shape of your sail thereby moving the center of effort aft. The increased wind speed will also cause a shift in the direction of your apparent wind (remember?). As a result, you will be sheeted in too hard for the new apparent wind.

THE SLAM DUNK

♫ THE BIRDS ARE CHIRPING
THE GRASS IS GREEN
I'M SO HAPPY
ISN'T LIFE KEEN ♫

AS A RESULT OF THE CHANGE IN APPARENT WIND THE CENTER OF EFFORT MOVES AFT

CE

WIND

GUST CAUSES SHIFT IN YOUR APPARENT WIND

STEP # 1

YOU'RE SAILING HAPPILY TO WINDWARD. YOU'VE GOT A GOOD JOB, A GREAT FAMILY AND LIFE IS GENERALLY ROSY.

With the center of effort too far aft, the board will round up sharply to windward. If the round up is severe enough to steer the bow through the direction of the oncoming wind, the result is tacking without moving to the other side of the board. Trouble in Dodge!

The other way to do a slam dunk is to encounter a header so severe that the wind actually shifts to the other side of the sail. This sometimes happens in the extremely gusty, shifty conditions you encounter on inland lakes and reservoirs. It's fairly rare if there aren't large land forms around to disturb the flow of the wind.

The rest is academic. The result is one big kersplash and snickers from the onlookers.

AVOIDING THE SLAM DUNK:

Your main weapon in avoiding the slam dunk is anticipation. Try to look ahead for changes in the water's surface which would indicate an approaching gust. The water will usually appear a little darker and be broken into smaller wavelets where the wind is stronger.

When the gust hits, you have to get the rig forward. The motion you use to handle gusts—sheet out, rig forward and to windward, lean, sheet in—will work fine. However, try not to let the sail luff too much because the center of effort of a luffing sail moves aft so your problem is compounded. If you react a little late you might stall the board and then you'll have to deal with that (see pg. 57).

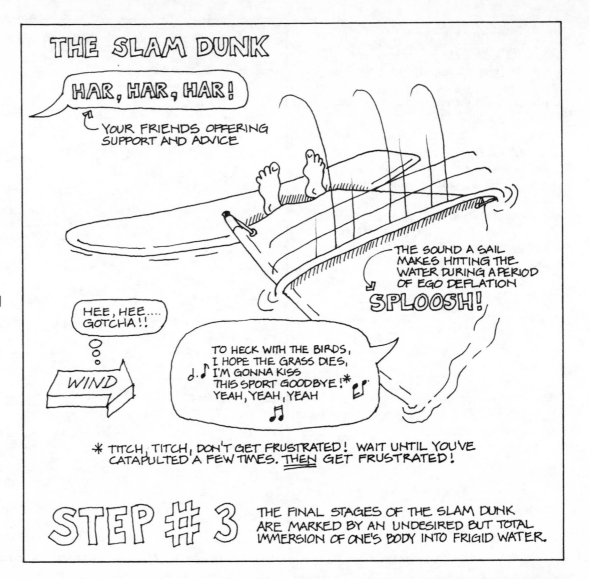

Zen and the Art of Windsurfing

BASIC MANEUVERS: UNINTENDED:

2) The Catapult: Sometimes referred to as "getting launched," the catapult is undoubtedly the most spectacular way of leaving a sailboard. The theory behind the catapult is this: As you are reaching and either attempt to steer to leeward or are hit by a gust, changing flow separation on the leeward side of the sail causes the center of effort to shift suddenly and dramatically forward. As a result, you are caught off-balance and the power of the sail is transferred to your arms, through your body and down to the tippy toes of your feet; which usually have no option but to become airborne. The fact behind the catapult is that it feels like Godzilla is trying to rip the boom out of your hands. It's really an unmistakable sensation.

You won't get catapulted in light wind but in anything above ten or twelve knots the whole process will become painfully self apparent. As with the slam dunk, you begin this maneuver blissfully ignorant of the impending disaster.

When your apparent wind shifts, your sail can stall which, in turn, changes the direction of the CE and moves the CE forward of the CLR (see pg. 27). When this happens, the pull of the sail will increase quickly and dramatically.

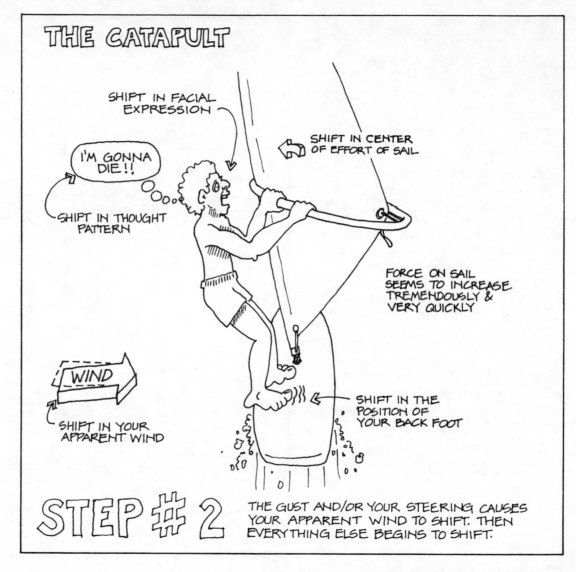

THE CATAPULT

SHIFT IN FACIAL EXPRESSION

SHIFT IN CENTER OF EFFORT OF SAIL

I'M GONNA DIE!!

SHIFT IN THOUGHT PATTERN

FORCE ON SAIL SEEMS TO INCREASE TREMENDOUSLY & VERY QUICKLY

WIND

SHIFT IN YOUR APPARENT WIND

SHIFT IN THE POSITION OF YOUR BACK FOOT

STEP # 2

THE GUST AND/OR YOUR STEERING CAUSES YOUR APPARENT WIND TO SHIFT. THEN EVERYTHING ELSE BEGINS TO SHIFT.

As with other unintended maneuvers, the way you finish a catapult is up to personal preference. Don't take catapult falls too lightly, however, because you can get hurt doing them. Also, it's on catapult falls that the rig is most likely to separate from the board, so be sure to attach your tether line!

AVOIDING THE CATAPULT:

As with the slam dunk, anticipation is your best weapon against the catapult. Unfortunately, it's harder to see approaching gusts when you're reaching. When the gust does hit, you must react quickly. The problem isn't so much that you're overpowered, but rather that you're caught off-balance. When you feel the tug on the sail, sheet out, lean and sheet in again. If your board has footstraps, get your back foot in one. This will keep you from being yanked off balance quite so easily.

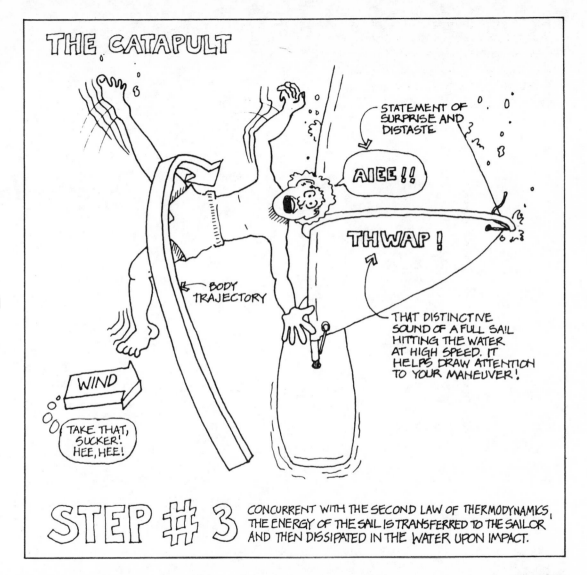

CHAPTER FOUR: GETTING BETTER

SO FAR WE'VE WORKED ON THE RUDIMENTS. YOU KNOW YOUR BASIC LINGO & THEORY AS WELL AS HOW TO UPHAUL, TACK & JIBE. NOW COMES THE FUN PART! SAILING IN MORE WIND!!

HIGH-WIND SAILING:
The speed and excitement of boardsailing increase tremendously as you begin to sail in higher winds. This is because the higher winds supply sufficient power to the sail to enable the board to plane across the surface of the water with greatly reduced friction and therefore greatly increased speed. And, depending on the type of board you're on (see Chapter One), at these greater speeds, the board actually becomes more stable and maneuverable.

Learning to sail in higher winds after having mastered sailing in light winds is often very frustrating since you feel as though you're starting over at the beginning. Not true!! You need to start in light winds and then advance to heavier winds. Everything still applies but you have to learn a little more. Some people give up after their first fruitless attempt in high winds. You should promise yourself right now that you won't give up until you've been on just one screaming reach with spray flying and the water whizzing by at an incredible rate. Once you do that, you'll be hooked for life!

SPECIAL PRECAUTIONS
All the precautions from Chapter 3 apply to learning in high winds but two points should be emphasized. First, never go out without your mast very firmly attached or tethered to your board. If your board doesn't have a tether and there is any chance of the rig coming loose from the board, rig a tether with a three foot length of strong cord or line. Simply connect any non-rotating portion of the mast foot to the daggerboard handle with the cord.

Second, don't underestimate the fatigue factor. Until you get pretty good, sailing in high winds is much more fatiguing than light-wind sailing. Fatigue can compound hypothermia problems. Don't sail too far from shore at first and don't be embarassed to ask for help.

Another good idea is to increase your self-sufficiency on the water by carrying some extra line and possibly some small tools or a pocket knife with you so that you're better prepared to deal with minor emergencies.

SPECIAL PROBLEMS:

Sailing in higher winds has some special problems associated with it. One of them is a much greater tendency to round up and stall out when sheeting in on the uphaul. We've said it before, but now it's more important than ever: RIG FORWARD AND TO WINDWARD as you LEAN and sheet in!! Exaggerate the forward and to-windward motion. Really lean!! Don't be timid, or you'll spend a lot of time swimming!

Once you get the board going on a reach, if the wind is blowing hard enough, you will almost immediately start to plane. Here we encounter problem number two. As soon as you begin to plane, the conditions affecting the way the board moves through the water change drastically. First, your speed increases dramatically and, hence, so does your induced and apparent wind. The result is like being headed so you'll have to sheet in hard. Also, as the board begins to plane, a large portion of the front of it will lift out of the water. As a result, the center of lateral resistance of the board will move aft. You must counter this by simultaneously raking the rig aft. If you don't understand the theory, don't worry about it. Just remember: SHEET IN AND RIG AFT AS YOU START TO PLANE.

As you rake the rig aft and sheet in, the foot of the sail will get quite close to the board. If you have the correct type of sail (RAF or camber-induced with a large foot) and you've rigged it as low as possible on the mast, you'll be able to "close the gap" by almost touching the foot of the sail to the board. This reduces the air flow under the sail (in aerodynamic terms, it reduces the spanwise flow) and greatly increases the sail's aerodynamic efficiency. The result is a faster, more powerful sail. If, when you attempt to close the gap, the board rounds up, your sail is probably rigged too high on the mast.

Once you get the board planing, you might encounter something called "railing." You will recognize it as a tendency of the board to turns up on its edge and steer erratically. This is caused by asymmetrical hydrodynamic flow over the daggerboard which causes the daggerboard to develop a high- and low-pressure side just like an airplane wing. When this happens, the daggerboard tries to lift itself right out of the water, railing the board in the process (fig. 86).

Usually, to remedy railing problems, you'll have to adjust the daggerboard position. If you're sailing a newer-style board, this probably just means kicking the centerboard up into the board. If you have an old-style board, you'll have

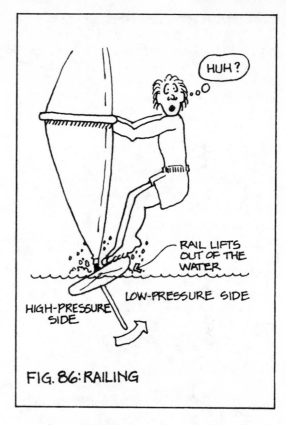

FIG. 86: RAILING

to release the boom with your back hand, reach down and pull the daggerboard out. You can either leave it partially withdrawn in the daggerboard well or sail while holding it in your back hand.

Another high-wind induced problem is that of being overpowered. This happens when you just plain have too big a sail for the conditions. You'll recognize this state because the rig will require an inordinate amount of strength to maneuver and control and you'll feel like you're always on the verge of going wildly out of control, which, in fact, you'll probably do quite a bit. The solution? Rig a smaller sail, or you can try to "de-power" your sail by doing the Godzilla number on the outhaul and downhaul.

"Spin-out" is yet another high-wind problem you'll encounter. Caused by skeg ventilation (often erroneously called cavitation) and/or skeg stall, spin-out results when the skeg loses its ability to develop lift and therefore loses its directional stability. When it happens, it'll feel like you lost your skeg. The nose of the board will spin into the wind, the board will begin to slide sideways through the water and you'll end up stretched out with your boom at your neck and your back almost in the water.

To avoid spin-out, get used to keeping your knees bent and the tail of the board beneath you. The natural tendency of pushing the board away from you with your feet can increase the skeg's angle of attack and cause it to stall. Also, unweight the tail of your board and pull it beneath you as you pass over choppy water. This will reduce the possibility of skeg ventilation.

To recover from a spin-out in the early stages, try sinking your leeward rail with foot pressure. Be forewarned, however, because this can occasionally cause you to bury the rail and do what survivors of the maneuver call the "warp-factor-six face plant." If sinking the rail doesn't work, try weighting and unweighting the tail of the board a few times in rapid succession. Recovering from advanced spin-outs often requires falling down and restarting. If you can, try pulling the tail of the board beneath you by bending your knees as you sink the leeward rail.

If you continually have spin-out problems, check your fin to make sure it's tightly fastened in the fin box. If not, shim and/or tighten it. If that doesn't help, move your fin forward an inch or two. You'll be amazed at how much difference these two adjustments can make.

SPECIAL EQUIPMENT:
High-wind sailing requires the proper board and sail to make it enjoyable (see pg. 9, Types of Modern Boards). Sailing a beginner board in anything over about fifteen knots can be difficult and frustrating. To keep your leisure-time stress level low, you should expect to invest in some new gear. At the very least, you'll need some additional gear to make your beginner board better for high-wind

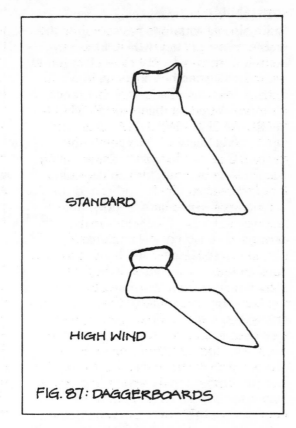

STANDARD

HIGH WIND

FIG. 87: DAGGERBOARDS

sailing. At the very most, you'll get a snazzy new board and three new sails. In both cases, there are certain things to look for.

First of all, you'll want a reasonably small sail. Something on the order of fifty square feet should do the trick for starters. Too big a sail will just make sailing in high winds a miserable experience.

It's also important to have a sail with a stable center of effort (CE). Old, baggy sails, and some new dacron sails, even if they are sufficiently small, can make high wind sailing difficult. This is because they are always changing shape which shifts the CE around. As the wind picks up, it'll feel like you're trying to hold on to a bucking bronco. If, during a gust, the CE shifts way aft, the sail can spin to windward, get backwinded and smash the rig (with you attached) down into the water. That, fellow windsurfers, is the advanced version of a slam dunk. Drag!! Generally speaking, fully battened mylar sails are best for a stable CE. But see pgs. 126-7 and 146 for more details.

Countering high-wind railing problems might also require some new gear. If you're trying to update a beginner-style board for high-wind use, you'll have to get a high-wind daggerboard. These are smaller and more swept back than standard daggerboards (fig. 87) and as such reduce the tendency of the dagger-board to rail by reducing its lever arm. Also they move the center of lateral resistance aft and this helps counter rounding up problems.

Another piece of high-wind equipment is the harness (fig. 88). This allows you to hook yourself to the boom in order to relieve arm strain. It's a nifty piece of

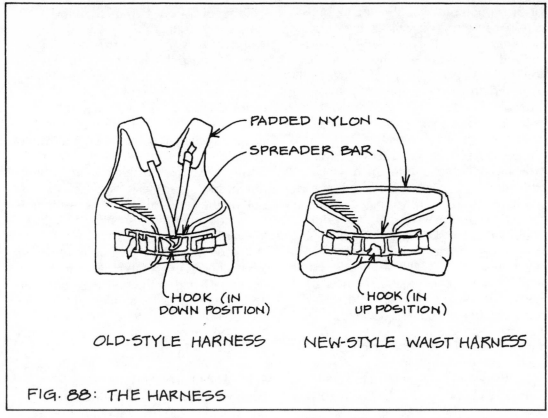

PADDED NYLON

SPREADER BAR

HOOK (IN DOWN POSITION)

OLD-STYLE HARNESS

HOOK (IN UP POSITION)

NEW-STYLE WAIST HARNESS

FIG. 88: THE HARNESS

equipment and once you learn to use it, you'll wonder how you ever got along without it. Instead of being exhausted after sailing for twenty minutes, you'll be able to sail for hours!!

There are a couple of features you should look for when buying a harness. First, it should be comfortably padded with good back support. Waist harnesses provide excellent lower back support and are popular because of it.

You'll probably want to get a harness with a "spreader bar." This widens the pull from the hook so the harness has less of a tendency to crush your rib cage on long tacks.

A great debate rages over whether it's better to sail with the harness "hook up" (with the open portion of the hook pointing up) or "hook down" (see fig. 88). Theory has it that you're less likely to do a full fledged harness catapult (see pg. 114) by sailing hook up. Practice has it that hook down is easier and faster to get into and out of so you may be able to circumvent even the beginning stages of this disdainful maneuver. Since the hook is almost always reversible, you can try it both ways and see which one you prefer.

A backpack-type zippered pouch is also a nice feature on a harness. It provides a place for car keys, a waterproof snack and your emergency kit.

In addition to a harness, you'll also need harness lines which attach to your boom and to which you hook the harness. You can tie these directly to the boom or use "tabs" which allow for easy adjustment and prevent excessive wear on the surface of the boom (fig. 89). You should attach the line just inside where you usually have your hands while sailing. For most people, this is about twelve inches back from the mast and another two or three feet back from there. When the loop of line hangs down, it should hang about twelve inches away from the boom. The actual use of the

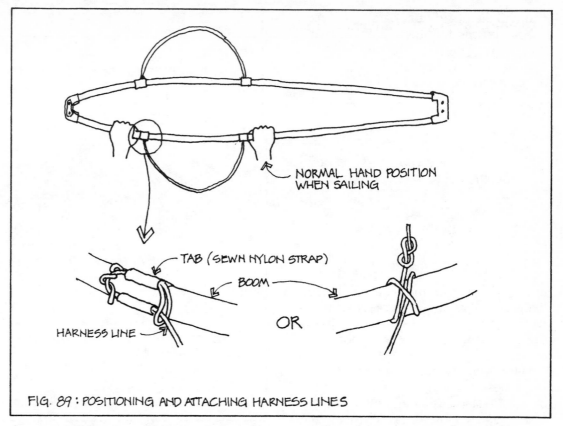

NORMAL HAND POSITION WHEN SAILING

TAB (SEWN NYLON STRAP)

BOOM

HARNESS LINE

OR

FIG. 89 : POSITIONING AND ATTACHING HARNESS LINES

harness will be covered in an upcoming section.

The last piece of equipment that's really helpful for high-wind sailing is the footstrap. The footstrap is just a padded loop of nylon or plastic attached to the top of the board. Usually there will be anywhere from three to seven footstraps

on a board. Getting your feet into the footstraps can have some real advantages. First, as we already discussed, it can help you prevent a catapult. Also, it can keep your feet from being literally swept off the board when you start plowing through waves at high speed. And when you start jumping the waves, it'll keep you and the board from parting company.

You can add footstraps to a beginner's board but by the time you need them, it's probably time to buy a more advanced board that already has them.

SPECIAL POSITIONS:

As you begin to sail in higher winds, you'll have to pay closer attention to where on the board you stand and how to adjust the daggerboard and mast positions.

Generally speaking, when you're reaching you'll want to stand aft on the board. This allows a greater portion of the board to come out of the water so the board will plane more efficiently. It also allows you to rake the rig aft and "close the gap" as we discussed previously. Don't, however, stand so far aft as to sink the stern. This just slows the board down.

When you are running or broad reaching, unless it is very windy, you won't be able to stand as far aft on the board as when you are close or beam reaching since doing so will tend to sink the stern of the board. In fact, running or broad reaching is pretty miserable in high winds, and it's nothing you'll want to do a lot. If, by predicament, you are forced to sail downwind in high winds, stand as far aft as you can without sinking the stern. Expect to fall a lot.

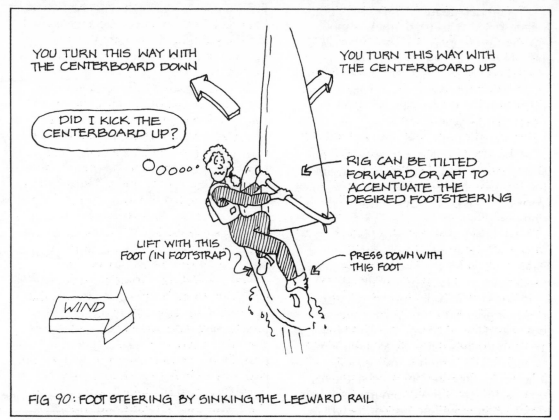

FIG 90: FOOT STEERING BY SINKING THE LEEWARD RAIL

When you're pointing, you'll want your body weight further forward. Your forward foot should be about a twelve to eighteen inches aft of the mast and your back foot another twelve to eighteen inches back from that. This allows you to sheet the sail more effectively and gets more of the board in the water which will generate greater upwind speed.

Your daggerboard position also depends on your point of sail. The daggerboard helps you point more effectively by keeping the board from slipping sideways through the water. So, when you're trying to point to windward, it should be in the fully down position. For close reaching you can try to leave it either partially or fully down until railing becomes a problem. For beam reaching and broad reaching you'll want it fully up or, in the case of centerboards (remember the difference?), fully retracted. Otherwise the board will rail severely and pitch you in the drink.

If your board has multiple positions for the mast or a mast track (a contraption that allows you to slide the mast step forward and aft while sailing), you'll want to pick the position according to the type of sailing you'll be doing. The general rule is that you want the mast forward for pointing and aft for reaching. If, however, you have trouble getting rounded up when you're reaching, try not moving the mast aft quite so far. Also, if the wind isn't strong enough to keep you from sinking the stern of the board when you stand aft, you might want to keep the mast a little forward. This will allow you to stand a little further forward on the board so you'll have a little more flotation beneath you.

SPECIAL FOOTWORK:

As you get better and the wind picks up, you'll begin to steer the board more with your feet and less with the sail. Footsteering is great fun and can be used to greatly speed up your maneuvers. You footsteer by purposely sinking one of the rails of your board with pressure from your feet. This effect can be accentuated by lifting the opposite rail by pulling up with your toes which are hooked in a footstrap.

Different boards will footsteer differently. The shape of the rails, the overall shape of the board, the board's length, skeg size and arrangement, and daggerboard position will all affect the way a board footsteers. Also whether or not the board is planing and whether or not there is enough wind to sustain a plane during the maneuver will affect the way a board footsteers. To find out whether or not your board is good at footsteering will require some experimentation.

The general rules for footsteering are easy. But, to make things confusing, there are two distinctly different kinds of footsteering requiring pressure on opposite rails in order to initiate the same turn. One type of footsteering is done on beginner-style flatboards and with the daggerboard in the fully down position. We'll call this "daggerboard-down" footsteering. The other type is done on newer-style boards with sharper rails and the centerboard fully retracted. We'll call this "no-daggerboard" footsteering.

Daggerboard-down footsteering is accomplished by controlling the high- and low-pressure sides of the daggerboard (see fig. 86). The general rule is that the board steers in the opposite direction of the sunken rail. So, if you sink the leeward rail, you steer to windward and vice-versa.

No-daggerboard footsteering is accomplished by stalling one side of the board by sinking it and letting the other side of the board plane around it. Hence it can only be accomplished if the board is planing to begin with. This is the type of steering that gives the water-ski effect of sharp turns and "rooster tails." The direction which the board steers is now the same as the sunken rail. So pressure to leeward causes you to steer to leeward and vice-versa. The faster you're going, the harder you'll have to sink the rail in order to initiate the turn, so don't be timid. We'll talk more about no-daggerboard footsteering in the descriptions of the maneuvers that follow.

INTERMEDIATE MANEUVERS: INTENDED

Now that you're a better sailor and you know something about high-wind sailing, we can start some intermediate maneuvers.

1) Beach Start: This maneuver, after you get the hang of it, is easy and flashy and will give you a feeling for how to do the all-important water start. To do it, you'll need at least eight or ten knots of wind. Be forewarned: During this maneuver the board will have an incredible tendency to round up. To counter this tendency, you must first be constantly aware of the board's and the rig's relationship to the wind. Don't get distracted and forget to check this!! If you have problems during this maneuver, check to see if you're getting rounded up without realizing it.

To start this maneuver, wade into knee-deep water and position the sail in the water so that the mast is approximately perpendicular to the wind and the clew is to leeward (see illustration). Get ahold of the mast about halfway between the boom and the top of the mast. Then just lift slowly and let the wind lift the sail out of the water. If the board wants to round up, get ahold of the mast even further toward the top of the mast.

Zen and the Art of Windsurfing

Raise the rig so that it comes completely out of the water and hold the mast just above forehead level. The pressure of the wind on the sail should keep the boom end out of the water. If the boom end keeps dropping into the water one of two things is probably happening. Either there isn't much wind or you're getting rounded up already. Beware!! There is a real tendency to round up during this maneuver!!

If you have hold of the mast high enough, you should have no problem keeping the board from rounding up. What you want to do now is to begin to force the board to leeward. Torque it to leeward by pushing with your hand nearest the boom and pulling with your hand nearest the top of the mast.

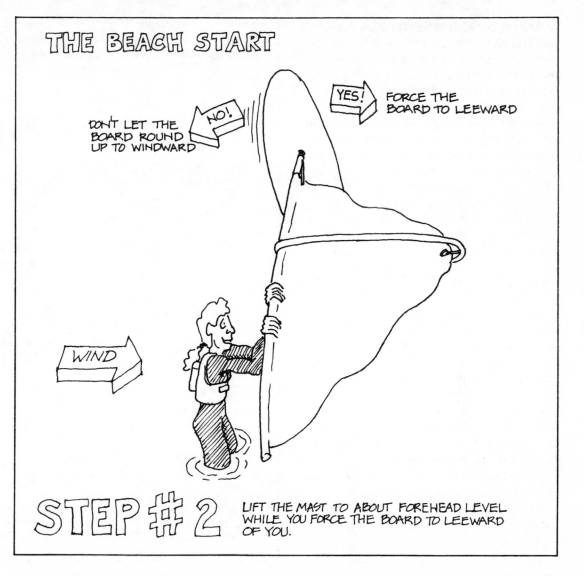

As you are getting the board to leeward, squiggle your hands down the mast until your lower hand is about a foot from the boom. Remember to constantly check your relationship to the wind. Concentrate on not letting the board round up. When you can keep it to leeward without any problem, transfer your upper (back) hand to the boom and get under the sail.

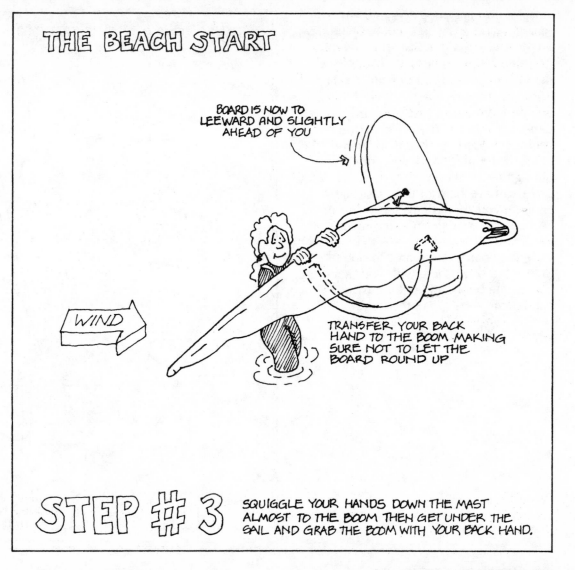

THE BEACH START

BOARD IS NOW TO LEEWARD AND SLIGHTLY AHEAD OF YOU

WIND

TRANSFER YOUR BACK HAND TO THE BOOM MAKING SURE NOT TO LET THE BOARD ROUND UP

STEP # 3

SQUIGGLE YOUR HANDS DOWN THE MAST ALMOST TO THE BOOM THEN GET UNDER THE SAIL AND GRAB THE BOOM WITH YOUR BACK HAND.

Zen and the Art of Windsurfing

Now you are under the sail. Did the board round up? Check your relationship to the wind. If it did, the sail will probably be pushing on the top of your head and you'll be feeling awkward and stupid. If this is the case, try to wrench the whole thing back to leeward with the boom. If you can't do that, the whole maneuver will self destruct at this point. Ah well, the most satisfying things in life never come easy! Back to the beginning!!

But assuming you can keep it from rounding up, the next step is to get hold of the boom with your other hand. Once you do this, you control the position of the board with rig position and sheeting. To keep it from rounding up, get the rig forward and sheet in. Using rig position and sheeting, keep the board slightly ahead and just to leeward of you.

THE BEACH START

ONCE YOU CAN SUCCESSFULLY KEEP THE BOARD FROM ROUNDING UP, GO AHEAD AND TRANSFER YOUR FRONT HAND TO THE BOOM

WIND

STEP # 4
KEEP THE BOARD TO LEEWARD AND A LITTLE AHEAD OF YOU WITH A COMBINATION OF RIG MOVEMENT & SHEETING. DON'T LET IT ROUND UP!

Next, get your back foot up onto the board. If the stern of the board has floated away from you, just walk directly toward it and it will swing around toward you. Then step up onto the board with your back foot.

With your back foot on the board, try to find a "balance point" which allows you to keep the board perpendicular to the wind with rig position and sheeting. Once you can keep the board approximately perpendicular to the wind, practice moving the rig and sheeting to steer the bow of the board to windward and then to leeward. Getting a feel for this balance point between the board and the rig is essential for eventually learning the all-important water start. Practice that balance point!

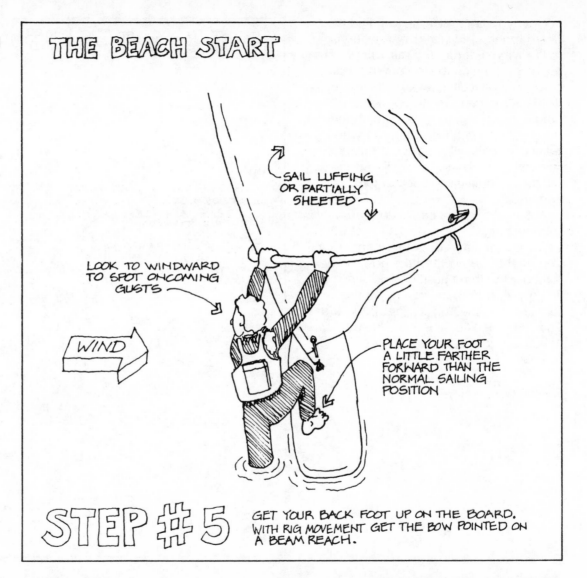

THE BEACH START

SAIL LUFFING OR PARTIALLY SHEETED

LOOK TO WINDWARD TO SPOT ONCOMING GUSTS

WIND

PLACE YOUR FOOT A LITTLE FARTHER FORWARD THAN THE NORMAL SAILING POSITION

STEP #5

GET YOUR BACK FOOT UP ON THE BOARD. WITH RIG MOVEMENT GET THE BOW POINTED ON A BEAM REACH.

Zen and the Art of Windsurfing

After you've found and practiced maneuvering around that balance point, all that's left to do is sheet in, step up onto the board and sail off into the sunset! Careful though, because a very common error is to pull the rig aft and toward you as you step up. This will cause you to round up and get dumped off. DON'T PULL THE RIG DOWN TOWARD YOU!! If the wind isn't sufficiently strong to pull you up onto the board, get your weight more over the board as you step up. If you keep getting rounded up as you step up, try raking the rig forward a bit as you sheet in. This should steer you down to leeward a little and help keep you from rounding up.

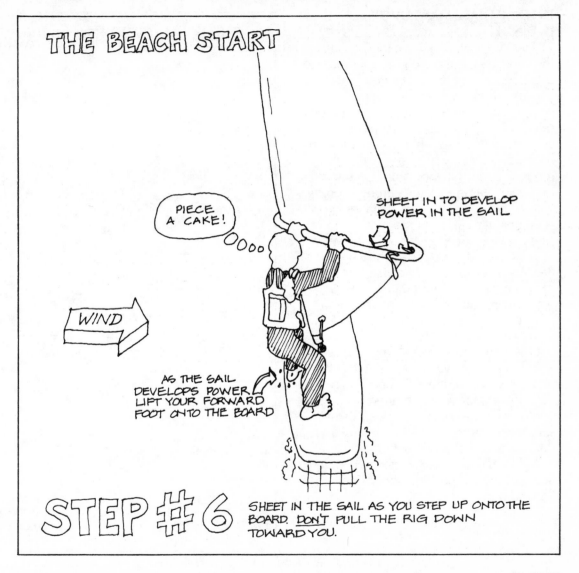

THE BEACH START

SHEET IN TO DEVELOP POWER IN THE SAIL

PIECE A CAKE!

WIND

AS THE SAIL DEVELOPS POWER LIFT YOUR FORWARD FOOT ONTO THE BOARD

STEP # 6 SHEET IN THE SAIL AS YOU STEP UP ONTO THE BOARD. DON'T PULL THE RIG DOWN TOWARD YOU.

INTERMEDIATE MANEUVERS: INTENDED:

2) The Water Start: This maneuver and the short-board jibe are probably the two most important maneuvers you'll learn in windsurfing. Water starting makes getting started in high winds and waves relatively easy. These conditions, of course, are the ones that make uphauling miserable. Once you've learned how to recognize the "balance point" required for beach starting, water starting is pretty easy to learn.

At first, it's easiest to practice water starts in waist-deep water. This allows you to get your initial position while standing next to your board. Of course, the whole idea is to be able to do them in deep water. For hints on obtaining the initial position in deep water, see Helpful Hints (pg. 97).

One of the most crucial ingredients to learning how to water start is sufficient wind. Twelve to fifteen knots should be sufficient for your first attempts unless you're fairly heavy or you have a small sail. Water starting in less wind is more difficult and will come with practice.

To begin, wade into waist-deep water and assume the position shown in the illustration.

THE WATER START

IMPORTANT! MAST MUST BE PERPENDICULAR TO THE WIND

WIND

STEP # 1

ASSUME THIS STARTING POSITION: MAST PERPENDICULAR TO THE WIND WITH THE BOOM LAYING ACROSS THE STERN OF THE BOARD.

Check your relationship to the wind. Both the board and the mast should be approximately perpendicular to the wind. Raise the rig by slowly lifting the mast (not the boom!!). This should be relatively easy because the wind will get beneath the sail and lift it. If you lift too fast, the sail will flip before the boom end has a chance to come out of the water. Nice and easy!

Don't let the board round up during this motion!! If you have to, wrench the board back to leeward the way you probably had to when you practiced the beach start.

Also, once you get the rig up and out of the water, concentrate on keeping the boom from dipping back into the water. If that happens, chances are the sail will fill, the boom will get ripped out of your hands and the rig will flip over. Bummer!!

THE WATER START

DON'T LET THE BOARD ROUND UP!!

NO!

BEGIN TO FORCE THE BOARD TO LEEWARD

YES!

WIND

LIFT SAIL

STEP # 2

SLOWLY LIFT THE SAIL & LET THE WIND GET BENEATH IT. IF YOU LIFT TOO FAST THE RIG WILL FLIP & END UP CLEW TO WINDWARD.

Force the board to leeward of you with the mast just like in the beach start. Then get under the sail and grab the boom in the normal sailing position. Don't let the board round up!! Wrench it back to leeward if you have to!!

Now is when the beach-start practice comes into play. Go ahead and find that balance point where you can control the board with rig movement and sheeting. Once you do that, mastering this maneuver becomes easy. Find that balance point!!

If the tail of the board floats away from you, don't worry about it. As with the beach start, a few steps toward it will cause it to swing in your direction. The important thing is that you find that balance point and with it you are able to keep the board to leeward and slightly ahead of you.

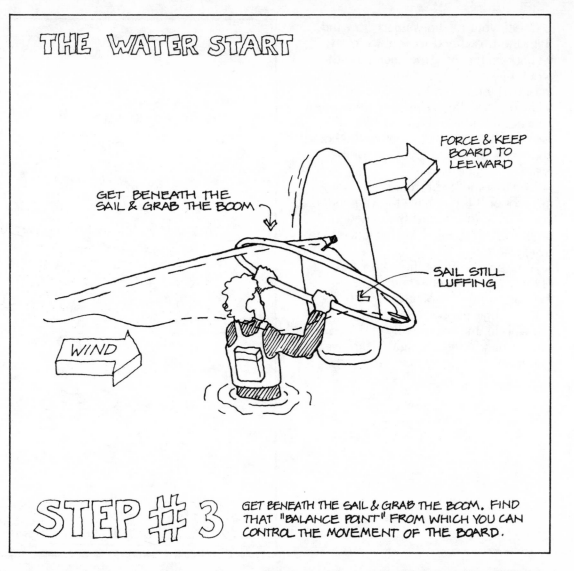

THE WATER START

FORCE & KEEP BOARD TO LEEWARD

GET BENEATH THE SAIL & GRAB THE BOOM

SAIL STILL LUFFING

WIND

STEP # 3

GET BENEATH THE SAIL & GRAB THE BOOM. FIND THAT "BALANCE POINT" FROM WHICH YOU CAN CONTROL THE MOVEMENT OF THE BOARD.

When you're confidently at that balance point, swing your feet up on the board. This may require some unceremonious kicking and thrashing about. If you want, you can sheet in a little. This will cause the sail to lift you a little and get you closer to the board. If the sail develops too much power, remember that the way to depower a sail is to sheet out. This applies for the rest of the maneuver: If you start to get overpowered, ease out with your back hand. Let go completely if need be. Never ease or release with your forward hand, however, or you'll go straight into catapult mode and the boom will get ripped out of your hands.

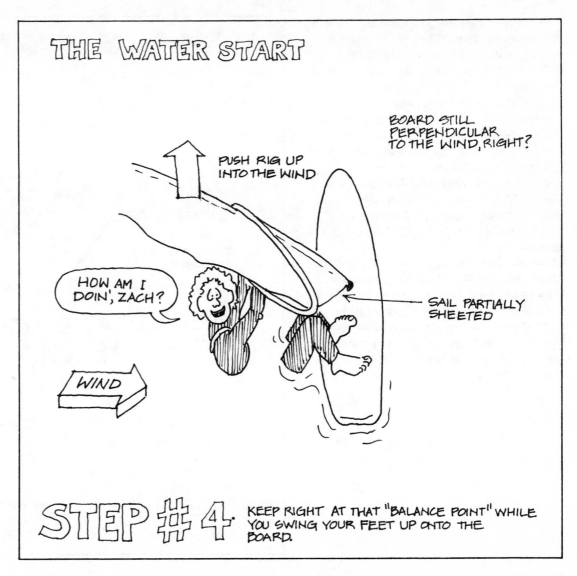

With your feet up on the board, sheet in and you'll start sailing. It's important to realize that you are indeed sailing at this point and even though your butt is dragging in the water, you can control the board with the appropriate rig movement and sheeting combination. Use this to keep at that balance point: Rake the rig forward to steer to leeward and aft to steer to windward.

On your first attempts, just sail along like this for a little bit. Then, when you feel confident, sheet in a little harder and let the sail begin to pull you up out of the water.

As you are doing this, try to keep your knees bent so the board stays close to your body. If you extend your legs, you'll force the board into a stalled position. No big problem, but it takes more wind to get you up in this position and then you'll have to deal with a stall once you are up.

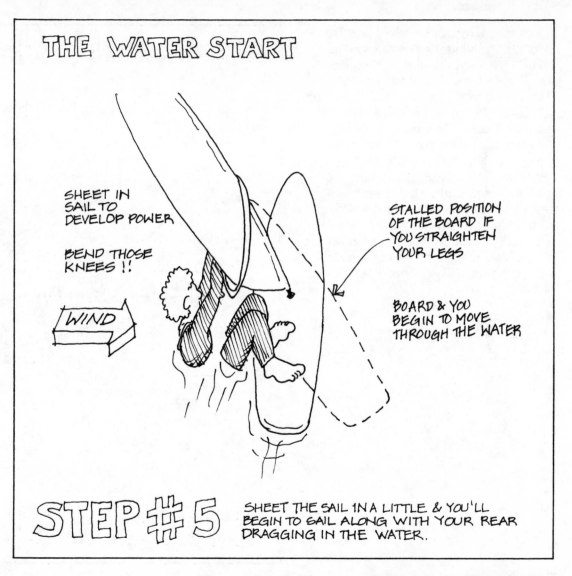

THE WATER START

SHEET IN
SAIL TO
DEVELOP POWER

BEND THOSE
KNEES !!

WIND

STALLED POSITION
OF THE BOARD IF
YOU STRAIGHTEN
YOUR LEGS

BOARD & YOU
BEGIN TO MOVE
THROUGH THE WATER

STEP # 5

SHEET THE SAIL IN A LITTLE & YOU'LL
BEGIN TO SAIL ALONG WITH YOUR REAR
DRAGGING IN THE WATER.

Continue sheeting in and letting the sail pull you out of the water. Get the board beneath your rear by bending your knees!! And keep that boom end out of the water!!

If there isn't enough wind to pull you up, push the rig up as high as possible by fully extending your arms. At the same time, pull the board beneath your butt by bending your knees. If that doesn't work and everything else seems to be under control, you'll just have to wait for more wind.

Assuming there is enough wind, it's still important to remember that you are sailing. While your hulk is dragging through the water, it contributes to the lateral resistance of the board. As you are getting lifted out of the water, your center of lateral resistance is changing. To compensate, you must get the rig forward a little as you are lifted out of the water. If not, you'll get rounded up and dumped off. This is a very common problem in the beginning so beware!!! RIG FORWARD AND SHEET IN AS YOU COME OUT OF THE WATER!

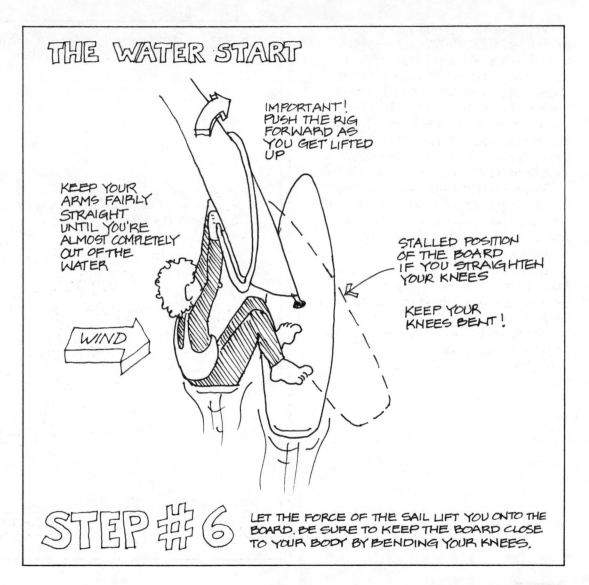

THE WATER START

IMPORTANT! PUSH THE RIG FORWARD AS YOU GET LIFTED UP

KEEP YOUR ARMS FAIRLY STRAIGHT UNTIL YOU'RE ALMOST COMPLETELY OUT OF THE WATER

STALLED POSITION OF THE BOARD IF YOU STRAIGHTEN YOUR KNEES

KEEP YOUR KNEES BENT!

WIND

STEP #6 LET THE FORCE OF THE SAIL LIFT YOU ONTO THE BOARD. BE SURE TO KEEP THE BOARD CLOSE TO YOUR BODY BY BENDING YOUR KNEES.

If you get everything right, you'll come onto the board in normal sailing position. And then it's off on a blazing reach!! Don't be discouraged if your first ten attempts end in failure. As with everything else, practice makes perfect. But you'll be surprised how easy this maneuver is after you get the hang of it. Three hours of practice in the right conditions will have you water starting and a week of practice will have you doing it like an old pro!

HELPFUL HINTS FOR WATER STARTING:
Although water starting really eases getting started in rough water and high wind, it isn't without its own trials and tribulations.

One of the most difficult things about water starting is assuming the initial position (see step #1) when you're in deep water. With the sail in the water, it is heavy and hard to handle. The trick is to let the wind do the work. Move the sail slowly and smoothly, letting the wind get under it and lift it and giving the water a chance to drain off.

For instance, if you fall so that the clew of the sail is flipped around the wrong way, just lift the clew a little and let the wind get under the sail. If the wind is strong enough for water starting, it should have no problem flipping the sail.

Okay, now you've got the clew pointed in the right direction. What to do next depends on if the rig is to windward or to leeward of the board. If the rig is to windward of the board (visualize!), you'll have to swim the mast around until it is perpendicular to the wind and the clew is to leeward. Grab the mast (NOT THE BOOM!) above the boom and slowly lift it out of the water. Slow and easy! Let the wind get beneath the sail and do the work for you. If you lift too fast or lift by the boom, chances are the clew of the

sail will sink causing the whole rig to flip around so that the clew is again positioned to windward. Just slowly lift the rig by the mast until the whole thing is out of the water and flapping in the wind. Then set the boom on the stern of the board and catch your breath before continuing.

If the rig is to leeward of the board (visualize!), it is usually easiest to obtain your initial position by dragging the mast and boom up onto the stern of the board (or, alternately, sinking the stern of the board and pushing it beneath the boom). The board's flotation will help lift the sail out of the water. The next step in the maneuver is to hoist the rig overhead. This is the time when you'll have the greatest tendency to round up. REMEMBER ALWAYS TO LIFT THE RIG BY GRABBING THE MAST ABOVE THE BOOM. Otherwise you'll round up first thing.

Once you're under the sail and have hold of the boom, you'll have to counter any rounding up problems by wrenching the whole rig using arm motion and kicking your feet. Remember that you want the board to leeward and slightly ahead of you so pay attention to the direction of the wind. Once you get the board in the proper position, you can sheet in the sail and move the rig to find that balance point where you can control

the board's position with rig movement and sheeting.

Okay, now you're under the sail and at the balance point. Where's the board? Very often you'll find it aimed in the entirely wrong direction. Not to worry! Just sheet in a little and you'll start moving! The pressure of the water against the skeg and daggerboard will cause the stern to swing toward you. This is true even if the board was originally pointed in the entirely wrong direction.

From there on out, it's just like doing it in shallow water. Sheet in, feet up, get lifted out, rig a little forward and blast off!!

WATER STARTING IN LIGHT WINDS:
Water starting in light winds is harder than when the wind is moderate to heavy. A couple of tricks, however, can make it a little easier. Once you get the rig overhead, always remember to push the sail up into the wind by straightening and extending your arms. If this doesn't help, quickly transfer your forward hand to the boom below the mast while the rig is in the overhead position. This both allows you to push the sail up further and gives the rig greater leverage to pull you out of the water.

Also, instead of putting both feet on the board, try putting your forward foot up near the mast and kicking with your back foot as you push the sail up.

INTERMEDIATE MANEUVERS: INTENDED:

3) Harness Riding: For harness riding you'll need at least ten to twelve knots of wind. It's easier to learn if the wind is steady. But then again, isn't everything!

From a normal sailing position the first thing you'll have to do is "hook in." The procedure for this varies according to whether you're sailing hook up or hook down. (see pg. 81). For hook up, pull the boom toward you. At the same time bend your knees and swing toward the boom. With a little practice, the harness line should drop right in the hook.

For hook down, sharply tug the boom toward you. This will cause the harness line to flip into the hook.

Unhooking is just the reverse process. For hook up, swing toward the boom while dropping below it by bending at the knees. For hook down, just tug sharply on the boom and the line should fall out.

Before you do anything else, you should practice hooking in and unhooking a couple of times. When you feel confident in your ability to do this, you can begin to ride the harness a little.

HARNESS RIDING

Y!!!!..

DOWN HOOK: TUG DOWN AND TOWARD YOU SHARPLY. THIS WILL FLIP THE LINE INTO THE HOOK

HARNESS LINE

UP HOOK: PULL BOOM TOWARD YOU AS YOU BEND YOUR KNEES. COME UP & CATCH THE LINE IN THE HOOK

STEP # 1

FIRST YOU HAVE TO "HOOK IN" WHICH IS EXACTLY WHAT THE TERM IMPLIES. THIS DIFFERS DEPENDING ON YOUR HOOK ORIENTATION.

Zen and the Art of Windsurfing

To begin to ride in the harness, just hook in and slowly ease the tension in your arms to transfer your weight to the harness line. Relax! Keep your knees bent and don't forget to look forward so you don't get in a wreck. Check for balance in the harness line. Are you hooked into the middle? Is one side pulling harder than the other? If so, make a mental note of this and correct it by adjusting the harness lines when you get back to the beach. Also check your distance from the boom. Are your arms fully extended? If so you'll want to adjust your lines so that the loop is a bit shorter. If you are close to the boom, you'll want to make the loop a bit longer. Usually, in the beginning, it's best to err on the side of having your harness lines a little too long. Harness lines that are too short make sail control quite difficult and sailing unpleasant.

HELPFUL HINTS FOR HARNESS RIDING:

When you are harness riding, it is important to realize that you are now lashed to the rig. Whatever it does, you do, including some fairly nasty things (see Intermediate Maneuvers: Unintended). Controlling the rig so that it doesn't do nasty things becomes something you want to know about.

One of the most important things you'll have to learn about harness riding is how to depower the rig. Up to now, that was just a matter of sheeting out with your back hand. When you're in the harness, however, this doesn't work because the harness line prevents the the sail from sheeting out. Instead, depowering the rig when you're in the harness requires that you slide the harness line aft in the hook. Your body position won't change much but sliding the whole rig aft will allow you to unsheet the sail. This is an important maneuver.

So, when you're harness riding, the old sheet out, lean, sheet in maneuver becomes a matter of sliding the rig aft, leaning and then getting the rig forward and sheeting in again. It's something you'll need to do a lot, so you'd better practice it before you really need it!

Changing course in the harness becomes a matter of gently swinging around. To steer to leeward, you swing gently forward and sheet in a little. Do this gingerly the first couple of times because shifting flow separation (did you read the section on theory?) can pretty easily put you into catapult mode. To steer to windward, you swing aft a little bit. After a while, you'll be using this swing technique to alter course as well as handle gusts and lulls.

INTERMEDIATE MANEUVERS:
INTENDED:

4) Short-Board Jibe: This maneuver combines the standard jibe with no-daggerboard footsteering (see pg. 83). It's spectacular to watch and lots of fun to do. It's also difficult and requires a lot of practice so expect to fall a lot before you get the hang of it.

You'll need three things to perform this maneuver. First you'll need the right kind of board. Either a high-performance "short" board without a centerboard or a "funboard" (see Appendix One: Types of Boards) with a fully retractable centerboard will do. You'll also need sufficient wind and sail area to have your board on a good plane. And finally you'll need fairly flat water. Learning to jibe in choppy water is hard.

The steps in this maneuver are almost identical to the standard jibe. The main difference is that you use foot pressure to steer the board and, in doing so, lean much harder into the turn.

When you're ready to start the jibe there are four things you need to do. First check to leeward. All clear? Okay, then kick the centerboard all the way up into the board. Unhook from your harness. Then take your foot out of the back footstrap and place it on the leeward rail. All done? Okay, now you're ready to start the jibe.

THE SHORT-BOARD JIBE

BEAUTIFUL BABY! NOBODY TO LEEWARD, I THINK I'LL JIBE!

WIND

SHIFT YOUR BACK FOOT TO THE LEEWARD RAIL

STEP # 1

YOU'RE SAILING ALONG ON A REACH, PLANING LIKE CRAZY: UNHOOK, KICK UP THE CENTER-BOARD AND MOVE YOUR BACK FOOT TO LEEWARD

To initiate the turn, sink the leeward rail with pressure from your back foot. Don't be timid! Accentuate the movement by getting your forward foot into a windward footstrap and lifting. The harder it's blowing and the faster you're going, the more exaggerated this movement has to be. If it isn't blowing very hard and the board tends to come off its plane when you turn downwind (which causes your apparent wind to decrease and hence less power, remember?), you'll have to ease up on the foot pressure and move forward as you turn. Otherwise, the board will have a tendency to track in a straight line along the sunken rail.

As the board begins to turn, be sure to lean into the turn. Don't be timid! It feels unnatural at first but once you get the hang of it, you'll really like it. Lean!!

During the turn concentrate on keeping the mast as straight up as possible. You can do this if the board planes throughout the entire turn. If, however, you come off your plane during the turn, you'll have to complete the turn by raking the rig across the board and forcing the rest of the turn with rig pressure like in the standard jibe.

Zen and the Art of Windsurfing

Keep the board turning until the stern has passed through the direction of the wind and you are "by the lee." Generally speaking, the less it's blowing, the more by the lee you'll want to drive the board before you jibe the rig. If it's blowing hard and you can manage to keep the board planing throughout the entire turn, you'll want to jibe the rig a little earlier. At first, try jibing the rig when you're about halfway between dead downwind and on a beam reach on the new tack.

About now, you'll also have to reverse your foot position on the board by stepping forward with your old leeward foot. At first, you should take a big step forward just prior to releasing the boom. This will get your weight forward so you'll have less of a tendency to sink the stern, round up and slam dunk on the new tack.

As you get better and faster at jibing, try not changing your foot position until after you've jibed the rig. The key to this is having enough momentum to keep the board planing while you jibe the rig and jibing the rig quickly enough so that you don't come off your plane and sink the stern of the board. The result is a picture-perfect, fully powered jibe. Yeah!

So pick your time, step forward and release the boom. If, when you release the boom, it feels like it's getting ripped out of your hands, you've sailed too far by the lee for the conditions. If, on the other hand, you release the boom and the sail blows out over the bow where you cannot reach it to sheet in on the new tack you've jibed the rig too early for the conditions.

Once you get the rig jibed, everything from the standard jibe applies. You have to get the mast forward and sheeted in on the new tack. If you managed to keep the board planing throughout the entire maneuver and didn't use rig pressure to complete the turn, then the mast will be pretty much forward when you jibe. If, however, you used rig movement to force the turn, when you jibe the rig, the mast will be way aft. You must get it forward quickly or the pressure of the luffing sail will cause you to round up and either stall or slam dunk. Get the mast FORWARD AND TO WINDWARD!!

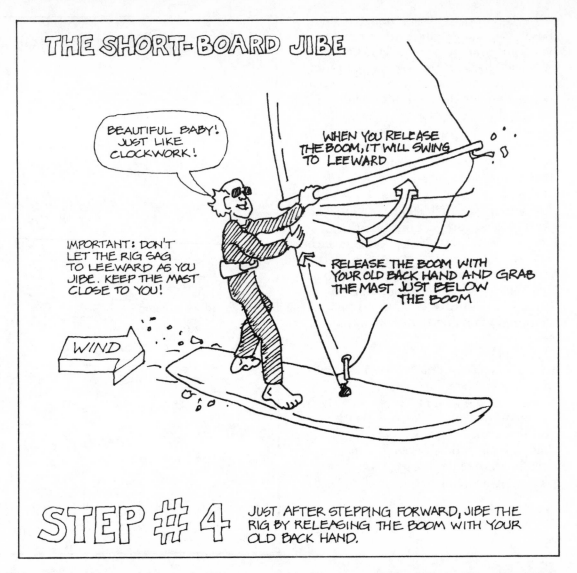

THE SHORT-BOARD JIBE

BEAUTIFUL BABY! JUST LIKE CLOCKWORK!

WHEN YOU RELEASE THE BOOM, IT WILL SWING TO LEEWARD

IMPORTANT: DON'T LET THE RIG SAG TO LEEWARD AS YOU JIBE. KEEP THE MAST CLOSE TO YOU!

RELEASE THE BOOM WITH YOUR OLD BACK HAND AND GRAB THE MAST JUST BELOW THE BOOM

WIND

STEP # 4   JUST AFTER STEPPING FORWARD, JIBE THE RIG BY RELEASING THE BOOM WITH YOUR OLD BACK HAND.

Zen and the Art of Windsurfing

Now it's just a matter of sheeting in on the new tack. Mast FORWARD AND TO WINDWARD, lean and sheet in. The harder it's blowing the more exaggerated your leaning and sheeting will have to be.

After you're sailing on the new tack, all that's left to do is transfer your forward hand from the mast to the boom. A good way to do this is to get your back foot in a footstrap and then hook into the harness line. Take the strain of the rig with the harness and then quickly transfer your hand. Be quick about it because, until you get really good at harness riding, you won't want to be sailing for any length of time without your front hand either on the boom or the mast. If you're not quite quick enough, you'll probably learn firsthand about the harness catapult.

INTERMEDIATE MANEUVERS: INTENDED

5). The Duck Jibe: This is one of the most beautiful and fluid maneuvers in all of windsurfing. As soon as you can consistently hit 80 to 90 percent of your short-board jibes, start trying duck jibes.

The main ingredient to a successful duck jibe is timing. It has to be perfect! The rig is jibed much earlier than in the short-board jibe. You don't sail by the lee at all but jibe the rig early and use it on the other side to drive you through the jibe. Most of the turning, however, is accomplished with foot pressure.

At first, you ought to practice the movements of the duck jibe on a land-based simulator or a long board in low winds but the real maneuver requires the board to be up on a good, solid plane, so you'll need fifteen or more knots of wind.

The duck jibe starts just the same as the short-board jibe: unhook, kick up the centerboard (if you have one), get your back foot onto the leeward rail and check to leeward for traffic. All clear? Initiate the turn by sinking the leeward rail and lifting the windward rail.

You have to keep the board planing throughout this entire maneuver so try to carve a nice, smooth but relatively tight turn. Keep that board planing!

Okay, here's where your keen sense of timing comes in. As you begin to turn downwind, your apparent wind speed will decrease dramatically. You've no doubt already noticed this on your short-board jibe. This is the time to jibe the rig! Don't wait!

To initiate jibing the rig, you release with your forward hand. Some sailors even shove the rig away from them with their forward hand. Either way, the mast will swing away from you. As it swings away from you, reach over your back hand and grab the boom near the end. If this feels uncomfortable, you can reach under your back hand and grab the foot of the sail near the clew. Whichever seems right!

But don't get so involved as to forget to keep the board turning!! Constant foot pressure!! If you don't keep the board turning and planing smoothly, your apparent wind will increase and the whole maneuver falls apart.

As the mast swings to leeward, pull the clew of the sail toward your head with your old forward hand (which is now at the end of the boom or on the foot of the sail).

Maintain constant foot pressure! Concentrate on keeping that board turning! If you stop turning or come down off your plane it's all over!!

THE DUCK JIBE

PULL THE BOOM END TOWARD YOU AND OVER YOUR HEAD

WIND

CONSTANT FOOT PRESSURE!

STEP # 3

AS THE MAST SWINGS FORWARD, PULL THE END OF THE BOOM TOWARD YOU. KEEP YOUR FOOT PRESSURE CONSTANT TO KEEP THE BOARD TURNING.

Then, in one flowing movement, flip the boom end over your head as you lean back and duck a little. As soon as the boom end is past your head, yank it down toward the water. This will bring the boom closer to you. Then reach out and grab hold of the boom in the normal sailing position. All the while, of course, keep the board carving smoothly through the turn.

THE DUCK JIBE

AFTER YOU GET THE BOOM END PAST YOUR FACE, PULL IT SHARPLY DOWN TOWARD THE WATER

LEAN BACK & DUCK A LITTLE HENCE KEEPING YOUR GENERAL GOOD LOOKS INTACT

WIND

GRAB THE BOOM WITH YOUR NEW FORWARD HAND

CONSTANT FOOT PRESSURE!

STEP #4 KEEP THE BOARD STEERING THROUGH THE TURN AS YOU FLING THE SAIL OVER YOUR HEAD.

As soon as you have hold of the boom with your new forward hand, release your other hand and transfer it to the boom in the normal sailing position.

If you've done everything right, you've completed the maneuver up to here while keeping the board constantly planing and turning. If you come off your plane or turn too far before jibing the rig, your apparent wind will increase dramatically making the maneuver next to impossible. The trick to this maneuver is to jibe the rig while your apparent wind speed is low.

Now just shift your foot position for the new tack as you use the rig to drive you the rest of the way through the turn. You're all jibed! If you did everything right, you never lost your speed and your movements were like poetry in motion. Beautiful!

INTERMEDIATE MANEUVERS: UNINTENDED:

Once you've passed the beginning stages of windsurfing most of your unintended maneuvers will involve the use of the harness. Two of the most common of these maneuvers are the harness jibe and the harness catapult.

1) The Harness Jibe: This maneuver is started just like the standard or short-board jibe. The main difference is that once you are totally committed to completing the maneuver, you discover to your displeasure that you've somehow managed to hook back into your harness line. Jeez, this is your unlucky day!!

Let the rig jibe around as you normally would. Unfortunately, you'll be in neither the position nor the condition to sheet in the sail on the new tack.

AVOIDING THE HARNESS JIBE:
Some boardsailors avidly claim that wearing your harness with the hook in the up position keeps you from hooking in quite so much on the jibe. Try it and see what you think.

Also, you can buy some small elasticized lines which clip to your harness lines and keep them from flapping around quite so much and hence accidently hooking into your harness. They will also keep the harness lines from wrapping around the boom as much as they might otherwise do. Unfortunately they make unhooking just a bit harder. Alternately, you can buy very stiff harness lines which won't flap around so much during the jibe.

INTERMEDIATE MANEUVERS: UNINTENDED:

2) The Harness Catapult: This maneuver starts just like the standard catapult except that you're hooked in. You're sailing happily along then either a gust hits or you attempt to steer to leeward and you get overpowered. Then you're off like a cannonball!

This maneuver can finish off in various ways. One of the more unpleasant is getting pitched to leeward while being spun beneath the sail. You end up dazed, under the sail and the water, and tangled in your harness line. This is when you get to try out your quick release buckle!!

AVOIDING THE HARNESS CATAPULT:
To abort this maneuver before becoming airborne, you must depower the rig. To do this, you must get the rig aft and sheeted out by sliding the harness line aft in the hook. Then lean back and power up again (see Helpful Hints pg. 100). To abort this maneuver after becoming airborne, you'll have to count on divine intervention. Being on a first name basis with the deities helps.

CHAPTER FIVE: GOING FURTHER

SO NOW YOU KNOW YOUR BASIC THEORY AND THE MECHANICS OF ALL THE BASIC MANEUVERS. WHAT NEXT? WELL HOW 'BOUT RACING, FREESTYLE SAILING OR WAVE SAILING?

Boardsailing is a a sport that you can keep getting better at for years and years. After you've mastered the basic maneuvers and had a taste of high-wind sailing, you've really only begun to explore the possibilities of the sport. Three of the more popular possibilities are racing, wave sailing and freestyle sailing. These specialties allow you to test your sailing skills against the sailing skills of others and this is an excellent way to learn.

Unfortunately, each of these areas deserves a book all to itself. So in this chapter, we'll only be able to discuss the rudiments of each. For more info, you'll want to consult a specialty book or the windsurfing magazines.

THE RUDIMENTS OF RACING:

In windsurfing, there are several different types of racing. Each tests different skills and requires different kinds of sailboards.

Slalom racing refers to a type of short-board racing which involves all reaching and jibing. Typically the course will have only two buoys, neither to windward of the other (fig. 121). The race consists of reaching from one mark to the other, jibing, and reaching back to the first mark, and repeating this for the required number of laps.

Course racing refers to a type of sailboard racing where there are both upwind and reaching legs (fig. 122). The upwind legs test the boardsailors windward speed as well as his or her ability to tack the board. The reaching legs test reaching speed and jibing ability. As such, course-racing boards are built to go both upwind and downwind and are usually equipped with sliding mast tracks and retractable centerboards.

Racing is exciting because it not only requires sailing skill and speed but also proper tactical reasoning. Racing tactics have grown out of a complex set of racing rules which govern the rights and responsibilities of sailors when they are racing. Basically, all the standard right-of-way rules apply but a formal set of hails and replies governs how you ask for and receive the right of way. Often a sailor who is tactically savvy can gain the right of way and beat faster sailors by thinking ahead and planning his or her tactics.

Starting tactics are especially interesting because any advantage you gain at the start, you'll have for the entire race. Also, by starting in front, you won't have to deal with the turbulent air caused by sailors in front of you. Generally speaking, the best place to be at the start is at the starboard end of the line on starboard tack (fig. 124). Timing yourself to get there just as the gun goes off is hard to do, but if you pull it off, you'll control the entire fleet because nobody can tack onto port unless they want to dip below your stern. At the same time, nobody has rights on you. If you arrive at the line a little early, however, you can be forced by another competitor to cross the line early. Then you have to restart and until you do, you don't have any rights at all.

The thrill of winning a race is great indeed. To win, you have to be faster and/or tactically superior to everyone else. This requires endless practice, meticulous study and total devotion.

Unfortunately, only one sailor per fleet will actually win the race. Everyone else will have to settle for second or third and on down the line. As a result it has become a popular pastime among sailors to practice losing. This does not entail

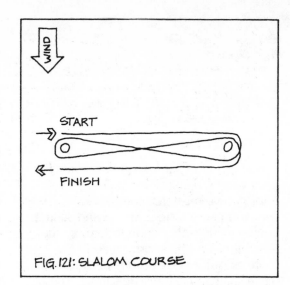

FIG. 121: SLALOM COURSE

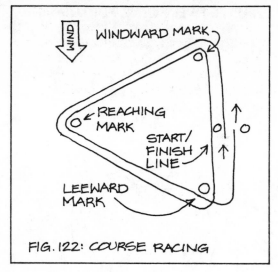

FIG. 122: COURSE RACING

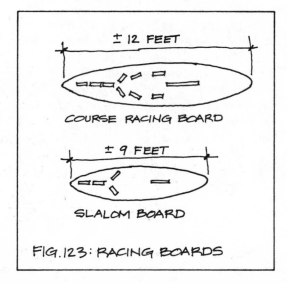

COURSE RACING BOARD

SLALOM BOARD

FIG. 123: RACING BOARDS

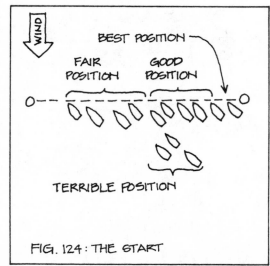

FIG. 124: THE START

attempts at deliberately blowing maneuvers or tactics. Rather, it involves finding excuses as to why you blew your maneuvers or tactics. This custom is sometimes referred to as "winning at the bar," since it is often practiced over a post-race drink (fig. 125).

FIG 125: "WINNING AT THE BAR"

THE RUDIMENTS OF FREESTYLE:

Basically, freestyle sailing is doing on a sailboard what you were never intended to do on a sailboard. It's a dazzling display of spins, twists, tricks and stunts. And it has evolved to be quite complex.

The actual competition is performed in front of a set of judges. Each competitor is given an allotted time period, usually three minutes, to run through his, her or their freestyle routine. The judges score the routine according to the number of freestyle tricks performed, the technical difficulty of each trick, the originality of the routine and the sailor's overall style.

Freestyle is fun to practice because it gives you something to do on those light wind days. The tricks you can do are varied and almost limitless. Some of the standard tricks are the railride (fig. 126), the head dip (fig. 127) and leeward-side sailing (fig. 128). You can even get fancy and use two boards! Experiment, invent some of your own tricks!

Since the freestyle sailor requires stability and not speed from the board, freestyle sailing is almost always done on large, stable, old-style boards.

FIG 126: RAILRIDING

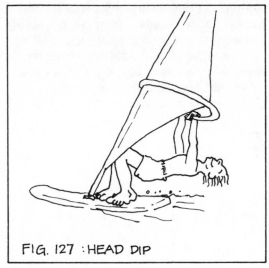

FIG. 127 : HEAD DIP

FIG 128 : LEEWARD SAILING

FIG 129 : USING TWO BOARDS

THE RUDIMENTS OF WAVE SAILING:

Wave sailing is exactly what the name implies. You need four things to be able to wave sail: a short and very strong board, waves, strong wind and considerable sailing skill.

There are countless maueuvers in wave sailing. One of the most popular is wave jumping. The four illustrations on this page outline the basic steps in jumping a wave. First (Step #1) you aim for the area of the wave just before the breaking crest. Actually hitting the breaking crest can result in costly equipment damage— not to mention the psychological stress associated with thinking you're going to die.

As you become airborne (Step #2), you have to get your weight aft and tuck your legs beneath you as you get the rig forward and sheet in.

Next (Step #3), you should extend your front leg to get the board set for landing. Don't plow in nose first, otherwise you'll be subject to more physical and psychological stress. Try to keep the stern of the board a bit lower than the bow.

And, finally (Step #4), you get to find out what the heck was on the other side of that wave anyhow! Happy landing and good luck!

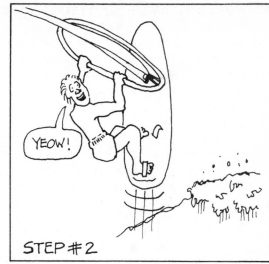

ZEN AND THE ART OF WINDSURFING:
So, here we are at the end of the book.
What have you learned? Hopefully a lot!
If you are proficient at all the maneuvers
described in this book and you understand pretty much why things work the
way they do, then you're well on your
way to becoming an accomplished
boardsailor. You've mastered the technique and now you can start on the art.
You can hone and polish your abilities
until you're a fluid example of grace and
beauty on the water. And one fast
sucker to boot! Windsurfing should bring
you years of joy, fun and excitement.
This is certainly my hope.

   May you always have white sands,
clear skies and steady breezes!

Good Sailing!

Frank Fox

Frank Fox

APPENDIX ONE: BUYING A BOARD

SO YOU'RE HOOKED AND YOU WANT TO BUY A BOARD! WELL, IF YOU'VE EVER LOOKED INTO IT, YOU KNOW THERE'S A PLETHORA OF BOARDS AND EQUIPMENT ON THE MARKET. WHADDA YA BUY? IN THIS SECTION, WE'LL BE DISCUSSING THE TYPES OF BOARDS AND RIGS AVAILABLE AND WHAT YOU MIGHT WANT TO BUY AS YOUR FIRST BOARD.

Since there are so many different types of boards and rigs on the market, it's easy to get confused when looking to buy your first board. Well, just to sort things out a little, we'll discuss the basic differences between the major classes of boards and rigs and what might be suitable for the conditions you'll be sailing in and your level of expertise. For a more detailed explanation of the performance characteristics of boards, see Appendix Three.

TYPES OF BOARDS:
If you look closely at a lot of different sailboards, you'll notice that they are really quite dissimilar in both shape and size. These differences (see fig. 134) affect how they move through the water, how they maneuver and how easy they are to sail.

One widely varying aspect of different boards is their respective volumes. The greater the volume of a board, the greater its buoyancy or flotation.

Boards are classed according to how much flotation they have. Those that can support a standing sailor and the rig while not sailing, thereby allowing you to uphaul, are called "floaters." A floater will typically have 150 to 240 liters of volume. Boards that cannot support the sailor and rig at rest are called "sinkers." These boards can only be water started and generally have less than 90 liters of volume. Between floaters and sinkers are the "semi-sinkers" or "bobbers" which can be uphauled if necessary, but which are easier to water start if there is sufficient wind.

In addition to the volume of the board, the overall shape of the board and the features it includes affect its performance. Most sailboards can be fit into one of six categories according to their shape and features (fig. 135).

First there is the "all-around flatboard." This is probably the type of board you learned to sail on. It's usually about twelve feet long and its wide stern, ample flotation and flat bottom make it easy and forgiving to sail. Some have centerboards which can be pivoted back for downwind runs while others have daggerboards which must be manually withdrawn. Their skegs tend to be small and they seldom come with footstraps. Also, their rails tend to be rounded which gives mediocre response to no-daggerboard footsteering and therefore mediocre high-wind turning performance.

"Division 2 Roundboards" are special racing boards which are unstable and tricky to sail. You probably won't want one unless you're really into division 2 racing (or log rolling).

"All-around funboards" generally range from ten to twelve-and-a-half feet in length and have enough flotation to be classed as floaters. They tend, however, to have less flotation aft, have sharper rails and a narrower stern than the all-around flatboards. These characteristics make funboards more maneuverable and responsive than flatboards, especially in higher winds, but also less stable and slightly more difficult to sail in lower winds. Most funboards will come with footstraps and centerboards as standard equipment. Some even come with a mast-track system. All the extra gear usually makes funboards more expensive than flatboards.

"Short boards" represent the funboard concept taken to an extreme. They are generally under nine-and-a-half feet long and, given sufficient wind, are fast and highly maneuverable. They are almost always sinkers or bobbers and require

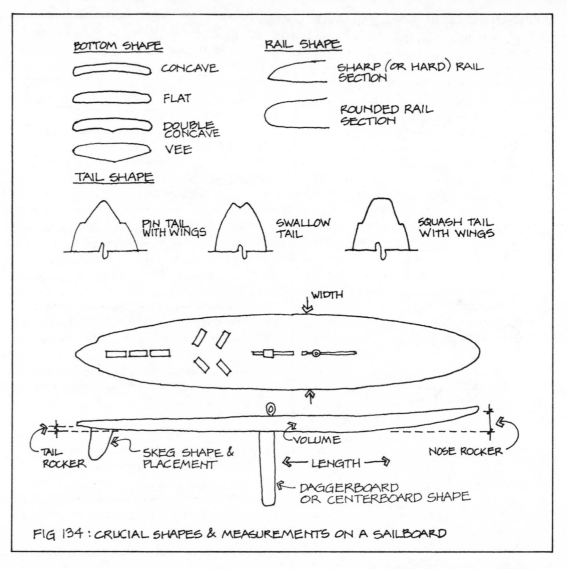

FIG 134 : CRUCIAL SHAPES & MEASUREMENTS ON A SAILBOARD

a high degree of proficiency at water starting as well as considerable sailing skill. Within the category of short boards, there are many sub-categories of boards. Two short-board types which you'll probably hear mentioned often are slalom boards, which are used for slalom racing, and wave boards, which are used for wave sailing and jumping. Each has specific design characteristics which improve its performance in its particular sailing conditions. Since short boards don't have daggerboards, they're hard to sail upwind.

Slightly longer versions of the short board, say 9'-6" to 10'-6", are called "transition boards" since people often use them to make the learning transition from a long board to a short board.

"Course boards," often called "race boards" or "Pan Am boards," are boards which are specifically made for course racing—a type of racing which involves both upwind and downwind legs. They're generally about twelve-feet long, narrow in the stern with hard rails, covered with footstraps, moderately difficult to sail, relatively fragile and fairly expensive.

"Guns" are boards which are built for all-out speed. They're generally very narrow in the stern, moderately short, difficult to turn and blazingly fast if there is enough wind.

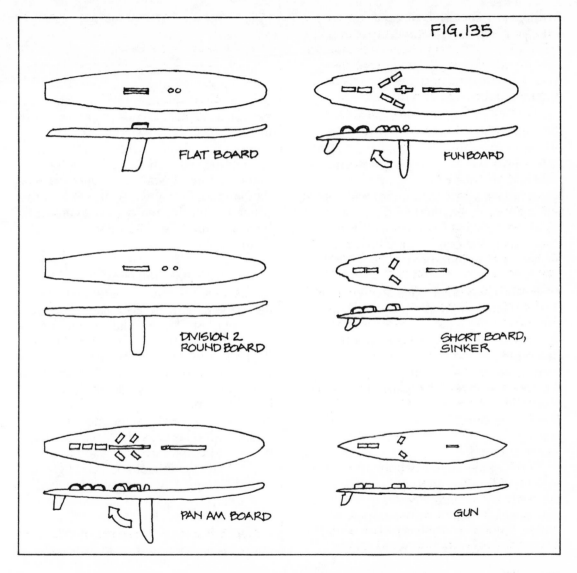

FIG. 135

FLAT BOARD

FUNBOARD

DIVISION 2 ROUND BOARD

SHORT BOARD, SINKER

PAN AM BOARD

GUN

BOARD CONSTRUCTION:

The methods and materials used to build a sailboard will also affect its performance. Generally speaking, the lighter and more rigid a board is, the better it will perform. Also generally speaking, the lighter and more rigid a board is, the more fragile and expensive it is. Builders, therefore, try to strike a balance between the cost of construction and the performance of the board.

In almost all cases, a board will consist of foam inside covered by a plastic or resin-based skin. The cheaper coverings are usually the plastic ones. Unfortunately, they tend to be flexible and relatively heavy.

Resin-based outer skins are lighter and more rigid than the plastic skins. They are also more expensive. "Custom" boards, those produced one at a time according to the specific wishes of the buyer, are generally built with polyester or epoxy resin and fiberglass cloth applied over the foam core. The polyester resin is cheaper and easier to work with than the epoxy resin but also heavier for a given strength.

Some of the higher-performance "production" boards, those produced in quantity by the larger board manufacturers, are built with a resin-based skin. Instead of the skin being laid over a foam core, however, the skin is shaped in a mold with the foam being injected afterwards.

The foam core of a board can also affect performance. Most brands are built with a polyurethane foam core. This type of foam, although relatively heavy, has the advantage of not absorbing water in case the board develops a crack. Polystyrene (also known as styrofoam) is used in the production of high-performance boards because is lighter than urethane foam. However, it will absorb water and for that reason, extra care must be taken when using a polystyrene-foam board.

MASTS, BOOMS AND SAILS:

Just as there are many different boards on the market, there are also many different types of masts, booms, fittings and sails available. Exactly what you buy at first depends a lot on how much money you want to spend. If you're serious about the sport, be sure to get an adjustable boom and mastfoot (fig. 136) which will allow you to use the same mast and boom with different sails. Make sure the boom end fittings are strong and that you can get the inhaul good and tight. If you plan to get RAF or camber-induced sails (see pg. 129, 146), make sure the boom is wide enough to accept them.

Also, get a good strong mast that's made for high winds. Cheap masts tend to break, rip your sails and abandon you to the fury of the ocean just when you need them most. Be sure to get a mast that's compatible with the sails you buy. Most sails are made to go on a fiberglass mast but many of the camber-induced sails work better with a stiffer, aluminum mast. The stiffer mast, however, won't work very well with the sails made for the fiberglass masts.

Sail sizes and shapes vary incredibly as do their construction techniques and materials. Generally, the best and most expensive sails will be made out of mylar or a kevlar/mylar combination while the less expensive ones are made out of dacron. Mylar is a superior material because it's stronger and lighter than dacron. It also stretches less. This keeps the center of effort (CE) from moving around as much when a gust hits.

The overall profile and size of the sail will also affect performance (fig. 137). The "powerhead" sail gives you additional area without moving the center of effort aft. It also generates more power high up in the sail. This can be a help when water starting in moderate winds. Powerheads gained popularity because they are "high aspect" meaning they have a relatively short boom for the given sail area. This makes them easier to handle on uphauls and jibes.

A relative of the power head is the fully battened RAF (rotating asymmetrical foil) sail. These sails have a specially designed mast sleeve which allow the battens to rotate around the mast when you tack or jibe. This makes the sail more efficient and easier to sail.

Camber-induced sails are like RAFs except that they employ an "inducer" at the mast end of the batten to lock the batten into a semi-rigid foil shape. Both camber-induced and RAF sails usually have a full foot which allows the sailor to pull the sail down close to the board in order to "close the gap." (See pg. 146 for more on RAFs and camber-induced sails.)

As a rank amateur, you won't want an RAF or camber-induced sail since their relative rigidity can be unwieldy at first. As soon as you start having high-wind sail-handling problems, however, you ought to try one. You'll be amazed at how much difference they can make.

The size of sail you want depends on your weight, your sailing abilities and the amount of wind you'll be sailing in. For an intermediate sailor of about a hundred and sixty pounds sailing in winds of around fifteen to twenty knots, an area of five to five-and-a-half square meters (53 to 58 square feet) should do the trick. Very large sails are usually for inland areas where it seldom blows very hard. Very

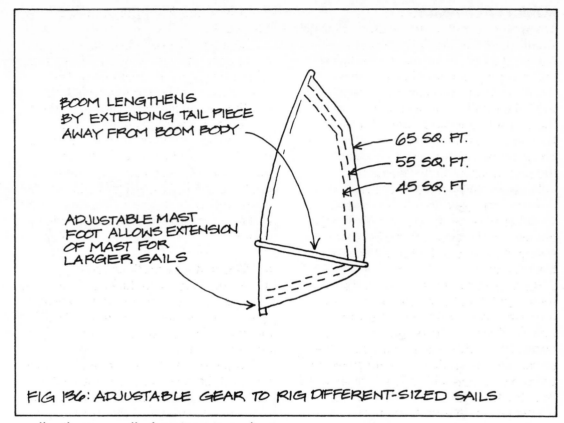

BOOM LENGTHENS BY EXTENDING TAIL PIECE AWAY FROM BOOM BODY

65 SQ. FT.

55 SQ. FT.

45 SQ. FT

ADJUSTABLE MAST FOOT ALLOWS EXTENSION OF MAST FOR LARGER SAILS

FIG 136: ADJUSTABLE GEAR TO RIG DIFFERENT-SIZED SAILS

small sails are usually for extreme conditions. A small sail, however, will make learning much faster and easier.

YOUR FIRST BOARD:

Okay, so much for what's available! What should you buy? Well there's no pat answer for that, but you'd probably do best starting out with either an all-around flatboard or an all-around funboard. Which category you choose (as well as the board you choose within that category) will depend on how serious you are about pursuing the sport and how much money you want to invest. There are advantages and disadvantages to both.

The all-around flatboard is the easiest to sail in light winds and the most forgiving and will therefore probably give you the most satisfaction in the early stages of learning. And, if money is a concern (isn't it always?!), you should note that flatboards are generally cheaper than funboards. The flatboard is also the type of board most often used in one-design competition and freestyle events. If you're interested in that kind of competition, check with local boardsailing shops and clubs to see which fleets are active in your area.

The all-around funboard is a little less stable in beginner's conditions and therefore slightly harder to learn on, but will give you more room for advancement as you get better. The footstraps, retractable centerboard and board shape will make your transition to high-wind sailing a lot easier. Funboards usually aren't

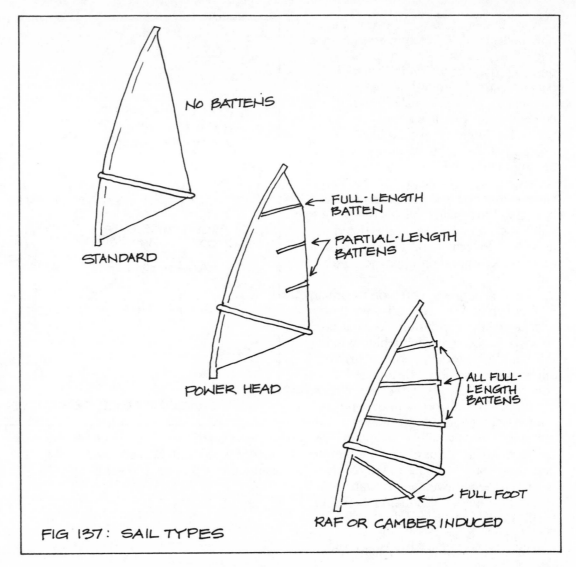

NO BATTENS

STANDARD

FULL-LENGTH BATTEN

PARTIAL-LENGTH BATTENS

POWER HEAD

ALL FULL-LENGTH BATTENS

FULL FOOT

RAF OR CAMBER INDUCED

FIG 137: SAIL TYPES

raced or used for freestyle sailing. They are generally more expensive than flatboards but, if you're sure about your interest in the sport, the extra money will probably be well spent.

In all probability, your first board and rig will come as a package so, once you've choosen the category of board you want, the decisions you'll have to make will be limited. Likewise, many of your buying decisions will be made as soon as you choose which brand name package you want. You ought to choose a brand name with a reputation for quality and resale value. Buying a cheaper brand that's likely to fall apart, go slow, or be limited to certain conditions doesn't make much economic sense. Look at the different brands and models in the store and then go out to the local wind-surfing hang-out and ask some owners of the same brands and models what they think.

But enough with brands and reputations, categories and classifications!! The most important thing about buying your first board is to actually get out there and buy one!! It's very easy to get over-whelmed by all the stuff that's available and you could spend the rest of your life going through the literature trying to figure out exactly what you want. Well, the perfect sailboard doesn't exist!! If you're in doubt as to what would be suitable, buy something basic and sail it for a season. Just make sure to get something with a reasonably small sail (55 square feet or less), a reasonably short boom (7'-0" or less), a strong universal joint and something which isn't so advanced that you'll never be able to stand up on it. By the end of the season, you'll be in much better shape to choose your next board.

A WORD ON STATE-OF-THE-ART EQUIPMENT:

When you go to buy a board, you'll probably find that you have a choice between the state-of-the-art, latest, coolest, fastest stuff and the run-of-the-mill equipment. Which should you choose? Well, while having the latest sailboarding equipment is nice, you don't want to spend a lot of money on equipment that is way beyond your abilities or that you'll wreck or will be outdated before you learn to use it. You'll probably find that there are never any really clear-cut choices. It's all a matter of weighing the pros and cons.

As far as sails go, we've already discussed the unstable center of effort (CE) problem (pgs. 70, 73, 126-7). Getting bucked around by an old, baggy sail is really miserable and frustrating. So, while a non-fully-battened smallish sail speeds learning, as soon as you start sailing in relatively high winds, you should buy a good, fully battened sail such as the RAF (rotating asymmetrical foil) or a camber-induced sail. (See pg. 146 for more on these types of sails.)

When buying your first board, remember that until you get pretty good at the sport, you'll tend to beat up your equipment. As such, it's best not to buy a fiberglass (custom) board or an epoxy-resin/polystyrene board since these are usually pretty fragile.

In short, just remember to temper your enthusiasm for high-tech, high-performance gear with the fact that it is fragile and expensive. Also remember that until you get pretty good, sailing advanced equipment can be difficult and frustrating. Don't buy something you'll have a lot of difficulty using! After all, you wouldn't buy a race car before you knew how to drive.

NEW VERSUS USED:

Buying used gear can really save you a lot of money, and, as with used cars, there are real deals out there. But there are also disasters, so beware!! Also, chances are when you're buying used gear that you'll be buying stuff that's somewhat outdated so don't expect the latest thing.

If you're going to buy a used board, you should first go to a few shops to get an idea of the type of board and rig you want. Shops also very often have bulletin boards where people advertise used equipment.

When you find a seller with the type of board you want, call up and make an appointment to see it. Maybe you can even make an appointment for a test sail. Be forewarned, however, that it takes a few days to get used to a board and get it adjusted to your personal preferences. If you've never sailed a particular model before, you might have a hard time at first. This isn't necessarily an indication that the board is a bad design.

When you're inspecting the board and rig, you should check for obvious signs of physical damage or general abuse. Inspect all the fittings closely for small cracks and splits. This means they'll soon need replacing. How about the sail? Does it crinkle loudly when handled or does it fold quietly like an old bed-sheet? The latter means it's "blown out" or stretched out of shape. As a result, it will be difficult to sail in high winds.

How about the board itself? Has there been hull damage? Are there cracks in the seams on the rails? Look for areas where the board has been patched. In boards with daggerboards, look especially at the aft end of the daggerboard slot. A patched hull isn't necessarily bad, but if water got into the hull and wasn't allowed to drain before the board was patched, it can cause the skin to delaminate from the foam core which can ruin the board. How heavy is the board? If it's very heavy, chances are the foam core is waterlogged. If this is the case, don't pay very much for the board because it's almost worthless!

Make sure all the pieces are there. Is there a high-wind daggerboard? A spare universal joint? Will the seller throw in a wetsuit or harness at no additional cost?

Inquire as to the history of the board. Has it been used a lot in high winds? What pieces have been replaced? Are the moving parts all gunked up with salt and corrosion, meaning the seller wasn't too keen on maintenance?

And finally, evaluate the seller. Is this person honest? Could the board be stolen? (If it is, you might just meet the rightful owner on the dock some day!). And, perhaps most important, would you buy a used car from this person?

APPENDIX TWO: MAINTAINING AND REPAIRING YOUR BOARD

SO NOW ALL YOU NEED TO KNOW IS HOW TO CARE FOR AND FIX YOUR NEW BOARD. WELL, IT'S NOT VERY HARD!

MAINTENANCE:

There are three major enemies you'll face in your fight to keep your board and rig looking and performing like new. These are sand, salt and you. The first two are pretty easy to deal with. The third can be harder.

The first thing you should learn is how not to be your sailboard's worst enemy. This is easier said than done because it's surprisingly easy to wreck your board. Always keep in mind that while sailboards are fairly robust, they are by no means indestructable. Fiberglass boards are actually fairly fragile. When handling your board, do so with care. Dragging it over rocks or asphalt can cause ugly scratches and gouges. Dropping it can cause dings and dents as well as holes and breaks. Be careful! If you're going to sacrifice your board, do it sailing and not carrying it down to the beach!!

Both salt and sand will prematurely age things and eventually wear them out. Your best line of defense against these two enemies is lots of fresh water and a hose. Unless you sail in clean, fresh water, it's a good habit to rinse your gear out after each use. Rinse off the board paying close attention to everywhere with moving parts, such as the centerboard well and the mast track or mast step.

Use the same approach with the rig. Rinse the salt and sand off the surface of the sail. Wash out the universal joint, the mast foot and any fittings on the boom. If you have an adjustable boom, take it apart and rinse it out. Watch for accumulation of sand in the mast sleeve of the sail which can cause a lot of wear when it rubs against the mast. Occasionally take the battens out and rinse them off. If there is any sand in the batten pockets, rinse them also.

And while you're at it, rinse off your wetsuit, your harness and any other gear which may have accumulated salt and sand.

Rinse that stuff! Water is cheap. Sailboards and equipment aren't. And besides, it's not just the cost. There's nothing worse than showing up at the beach when it's blowing great, only to find out that you can't go sailing because some three-dollar part is gunked up with salt and corrosion. Then all you get to do is watch everyone else sail and kick yourself for never rinsing your stuff off.

After you've rinsed your stuff off, you'll have to store it. If you're in one of those unusual crime-free areas where you have the option of storing your stuff outside, be forewarned that prolonged exposure to the sun can fade and ruin equipment. This is especially true of sailcloth and fittings like footstraps. It's best to store your stuff inside in a well-ventilated area so that it gets a chance to dry thoroughly.

The board usually doesn't present much of a problem. Just prop it up on some wooden blocks so the skeg or footstraps don't take all the weight.

The rig presents a little more of a problem. The sail should be allowed to dry. For non-fully-battened sails, this is most easily done by suspending it right on the mast somehow. If you hang the thing from nails, make sure the nails don't come into contact with the sailcloth. When the nails eventually rust, they can stain and weaken the cloth. Before you hang it up to dry, however, make sure that the battens are out of the sail and the downhaul is plenty loose. If not, the sail will stretch out of shape prematurely and you'll be off to the store to buy a new one sooner than you thought.

After the sail is dry, the best way to store it is just to leave it hanging the way it is. If you can't leave it hanging, the next best thing is to roll it loosely around the mast (downhaul loose, remember!?). And if you can't do that, your final option

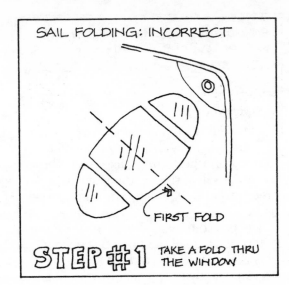

SAIL FOLDING: INCORRECT

FIG:138

SECOND FOLD

FIRST FOLD

STEP #1 TAKE A FOLD THRU THE WINDOW

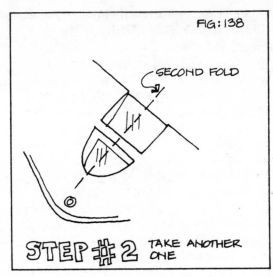

STEP #2 TAKE ANOTHER ONE

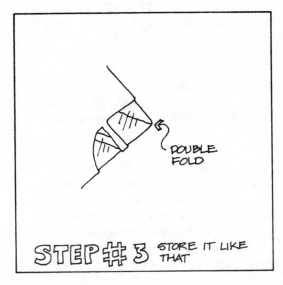

DOUBLE FOLD

STEP #3 STORE IT LIKE THAT

HELLO? ACME SAIL REPAIR?

STEP #4 EXPAND YOUR CIRCLE OF FRIENDS

is to fold the thing. There are many ways to do this and it really depends on the cut of your sail. The main thing to remember is that you don't want to take a double fold in the window of a sail (fig.138). Doing so, especially repeatedly in the same area, can cause the window to weaken and tear. In fact, you don't really want to take even a single sharp fold in the window but this is usually unavoidable. Most windows are sewn so that taking a double fold is avoidable (fig. 139). Once you get the thing loosely rolled or folded and in a sail bag if you have one, put it on top of everything else. Don't store heavy stuff on top of it because this will cause the fabric and window material to crease, causing it to weaken*.

The process for drying and storing fully battened sails is a bit different. First loosen all the battens, take the sail off the mast and rinse it off. Then loosely roll the sail starting at the head. Depending on the exact batten configuration, you might have to remove one or more of the battens in order to roll the sail. Store the rolled sail standing on end so it has a chance to drain and dry. Be sure to roll the sail loosely or it won't dry properly.

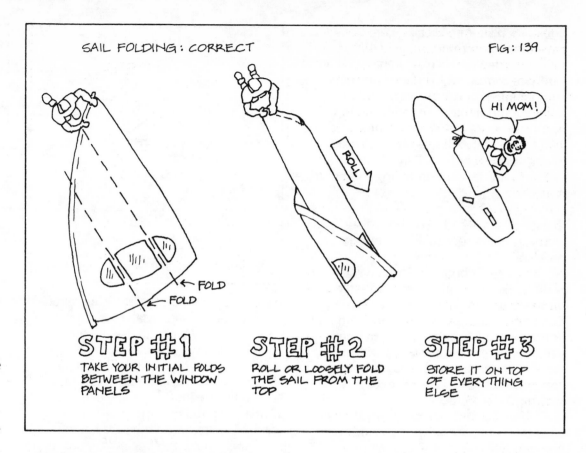

SAIL FOLDING: CORRECT   FIG: 139

STEP #1
TAKE YOUR INITIAL FOLDS BETWEEN THE WINDOW PANELS

STEP #2
ROLL OR LOOSELY FOLD THE SAIL FROM THE TOP

STEP #3
STORE IT ON TOP OF EVERYTHING ELSE

*Another note on sail windows is that they often shrink permanently when they become excessively hot. As a result, it is impossible to set the sail without massive wrinkles. So don't store your sails all day in a closed car on hot or sunny days.

REPAIRS (PERMANENT):

The repairs you undertake on your sailboard depend on how handy you are and whether or not you have the tools and facilities necessary to make the repair. Major repairs are probably best left to the pros. But minor repairs you can make yourself. And making the repairs yourself is not only usually cheaper but also usually faster than taking the board to a shop.

1) Hull Damage: One of the worst things you can do to your sailboard is to put a hole in it. Not just a ding or a dent or a scratch but a bona fide hole. When you do this, don't sail it anymore!! Water can leak in and wreck the board. Get it out of the water and attempt to drain any water which has entered. When you get it home, rinse the wound with a little fresh water and prop the board up so that it can drain. Leave it like this at least overnight.

The next step is to fix it or get it fixed. The procedure for fixing it depends on the material of construction and the severity of the damage.

Fiberglass boards are easiest to fix. This is poetic justice since they are also the easiest to wreck. Small holes can be filled with epoxy putty. To fix the hole, clean out any loose debris and roughen the area of damage with 80 grit sand-

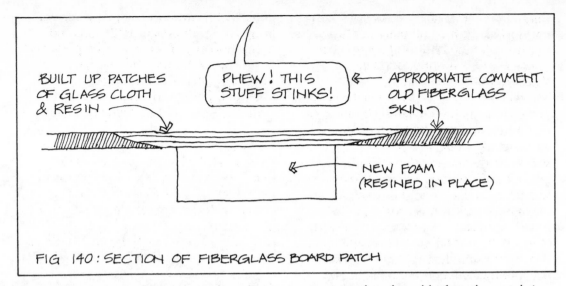

FIG 140: SECTION OF FIBERGLASS BOARD PATCH

paper. Then mix up the putty and apply it with a putty knife. Make sure to mix the putty really well otherwise you'll have a real mess on your hands. Don't build it up real high or it will be a pain to sand off later. Once the putty has cured, sand it flush with the surface of the board with 120 or 180 grit sandpaper. Then sand the patch smooth by graduating to smoother and smoother sandpaper until you finish with 600 grit.

Larger holes require some fiberglass cloth and epoxy resin. First grind or sand away the damaged fiberglass making sure not to put any deep gouges in the foam core. If the foam around the damage is water-logged, it should be carefully cut out and replaced before the patch is installed. The idea behind the patch is to build up the damaged area with layers of resin-soaked fiberglass cloth until it is flush with the surface of the board (fig. 140). First, cut your patches and then mix up your resin. Don't mix very much. Usually a quarter cup is more than you need but mix up that much so you get the proportions right. Soak the patches and squeegee out any excess resin. Then apply them sucessively, working out any air bubbles which might occur. After you have the patch built up high enough, let the resin cure and then sand it smooth. You might have to apply some epoxy putty to fill any small voids which still remain. Then apply a coat of "finishing" resin over the entire area with a brush, let it cure and sand the surface smooth with extra-fine sandpaper. Presto! You're done!

Plastic boards are a bit trickier to fix. The exact approach depends on the type of plastic and the extent of the damage. Severe splits and cracks must be repaired by a professional. Hold on to your hats when asking for a quote because this type of work is usually pretty expensive.

On most plastic boards, minor cracks or splits can usually be taken care of with epoxy putty or PVC cement. To make sure such substances will work, call up a shop that sells your type of board and ask. If they don't know, call up the manufacturer or the regional distributor. Usually they'll have someone on staff that can answer your questions.

Minor splits along the rails can often be fixed with PVC cement. It's available in most hardware stores so buy a small can of it and a small flux brush or paintbrush to apply it. Make sure the split is dry and free of any debris. Then apply a moderate amount of the cement to the edges of the split. Don't apply too much or everything will become a gooey mess. Then just clamp the split closed until the glue is set.

For other types of cracks or splits you'll have to use putty. First, remove any loose debris from the damaged area and roughen up the edges with some 80 grit sandpaper. Then apply the putty and let it cure. After that, all you have to do is sand it smooth using progressively finer and finer sandpaper the same as with the repair of the fiberglass board.

2) Mast Repair: Surprisingly, it doesn't take a lot of wind or big waves to break a mast. Most avid windsurfers (like you!) will one day find themselves with a broken mast. When you least expect it, it'll happen.

Fiberglass masts can be repaired. Aluminum masts usually can't. But before you jump at the chance to repair your broken fiberglass mast, make an honest assessment of it. Is it worth the time, money and trouble of fixing it? Would you do better by buying a higher-quality mast? Only if it has good future prospects should you bother fixing it.

To fix a mast, you'll need some epoxy resin (a one-quart kit will do six or eight repairs), some six-inch-wide fiberglass cloth (about eight feet for the average repair), 120 grit sandpaper, some surgical type gloves and some denatured alcohol for clean up.

The exact procedure for repair depends on where the damage has occurred. Usually a mast will either split at the base or break where the boom attaches. Splits are easiest to repair. First, sand the mast from the base to about a foot above the end of the split. This will promote good adhesion of the cloth and resin. Then check to make sure the inside of the mast is still round and will still accept your mastfoot. If not, you'll need to clamp it so that it does. An easy way to do this is to slip a hose clamp over the end of the mast and tighten it down. In a pinch, you could use wire twisted with a pair of pliers. Whatever you use, don't slip it very far over the base of the mast because you'll eventually cut off the end of the mast to get rid of it. Usually you can get away with losing only one-quarter to one-half an inch of your mast.

Okay, now you've got the split closed and you're ready to apply the fiberglass. First, make a dry run, wrapping the cloth around the mast to check exactly what length you'll need. The idea is to get the cloth to overlap so that you get at least three layers of cloth everywhere from the base of the mast to about eight inches above the end of the split (see fig. 141).

So make your test run and cut your cloth to length. Then mix up your resin. But first, open the windows because the stuff really stinks and isn't very healthy to breathe. You'll need surprisingly little. A half pint will soak ten feet of six inch cloth. Measure and mix the resin carefully and thoroughly!! If you don't, the whole project will turn into a nightmare because the resin will never cure properly. After you've finished mixing, pull on those surgical gloves, offer a quick prayer to the deities and proceed with the operation.

Roll the cloth loosely and then thoroughly soak it in the resin. The cloth should turn clear when fully soaked, so beware of any white areas. After soaking it, lay it out on some scrap wood or cardboard and squeegee out the excess resin.

Then wrap the cloth around the mast just as you did on the dry run. Work slowly and carefully making sure to wrap the cloth fairly tight and work out any air bubbles which might occur. It helps to have a friend to turn and steady the mast as you work. Re-soak any areas of the cloth which look a little dry.

After you finish wrapping the mast, work out any excess resin by wringing the patch with your (gloved) hands. Check inside the mast to see if any resin has dripped in which will later make getting the mastfoot in or out a problem. If so, remove it now with a rag. Then just let the resin cure until it's hard.

If you had to clamp the split, the last thing you'll have to do is hacksaw off the last quarter inch or so to remove the clamp after the resin has cured. Be sure

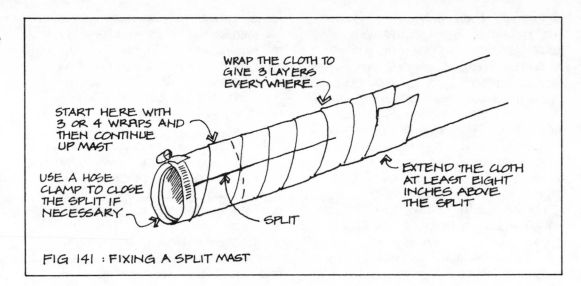

WRAP THE CLOTH TO GIVE 3 LAYERS EVERYWHERE.

START HERE WITH 3 OR 4 WRAPS AND THEN CONTINUE UP MAST

USE A HOSE CLAMP TO CLOSE THE SPLIT IF NECESSARY

SPLIT

EXTEND THE CLOTH AT LEAST EIGHT INCHES ABOVE THE SPLIT

FIG 141 : FIXING A SPLIT MAST

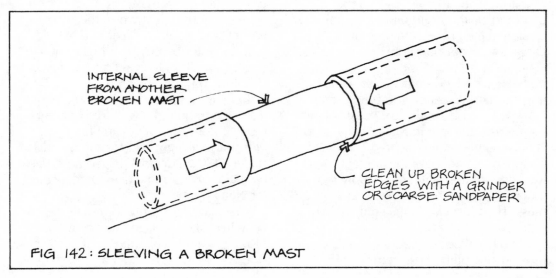

INTERNAL SLEEVE FROM ANOTHER BROKEN MAST

CLEAN UP BROKEN EDGES WITH A GRINDER OR COARSE SANDPAPER

FIG 142 : SLEEVING A BROKEN MAST

to make a clean and square cut. Finish the end by sanding it with some 120 grit sandpaper.

Breaks near the boom are harder to repair and more likely to break again than splits at the base of the mast. If you have a mast that breaks at the boom, you should probably chuck it and buy a new one unless you only intend to use it for light-wind sailing.

The process of wrapping and resining a mast broken at the boom is the same as for a split, but the prep work is a little more complex. The basic idea is to put an internal sleeve in the area of the break (fig. 142). This sleeve is made from the remains of another broken mast which you can often obtain from a boardsailing friend or a shop which does repairs. The sleeve should fit tightly and be res-ined in place before you patch the outside of the mast. To patch the outside you just follow the general procedure for patching splits. Sand the mast to promote good adhesion and then wrap it with three layers of resin-soaked cloth.

Always remember that a repaired mast is almost never as strong as a new mast and you should always test your repairs in light conditions before you sail in more extreme conditions. Never use a repaired mast in extreme conditions or anywhere its failure could jeopardize your safety.

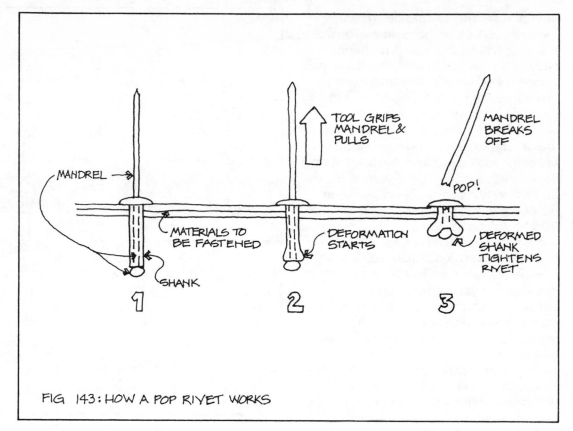

FIG 143: HOW A POP RIVET WORKS

4) Replacing Fittings: Besides repairing the mast and fixing holes in the board, the only other thing you'll probably need to do is replace fittings such as cleats or boom end fittings. One thing you should realize is that fitting sizes in the great world of windsurfing are not standardized. Even if the salesperson swears that the fitting you're buying will fit perfectly, you can usually count on shimming, filing, sanding and swearing it into place. For shims, cut-up aluminum beer cans work great. For sliding together tight fits, try some liquid soap.

Many fittings on a sailboard are held together with screws. Since we all learned in second grade how screws work, we can skip that and go on to pop rivets. Things like boom end fittings and some mast feet are pop riveted together. Pop rivets work by deforming part of the rivet so that it can't come out of the hole it went into (fig. 143). To remove a pop rivet you need to drill it out with an electric drill. Select a drill bit the same size as the original shank (usually 3/16"). If you're in doubt, use one a little bigger than the hole in the middle of the exposed part of the rivet. Drill until the head of the rivet comes loose and starts spinning with the drill bit. That doesn't happen? Go to a slightly larger drill bit.

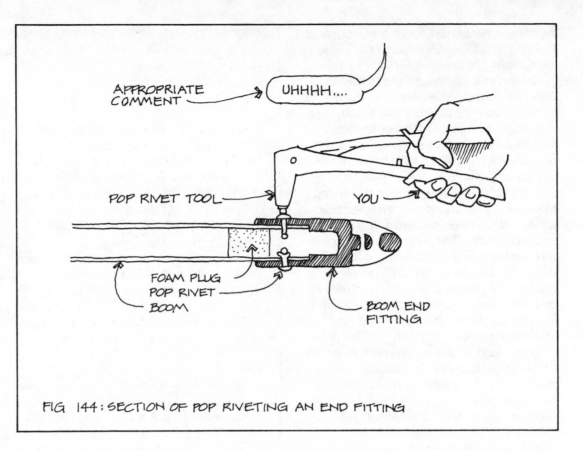

FIG 144: SECTION OF POP RIVETING AN END FITTING

Zen and the Art of Windsurfing

When the head comes off, the body of the rivet should drop through the original hole. Sometimes you need to offer some persuasion by hitting it lightly with a nail punch and a hammer.

To remove a riveted fitting, simply drill out all the rivets and pull the fitting off. To install the new fitting, simply slip it into place and re-rivet. (Remember the part about shimming, filing, sanding and swearing). If the original holes don't align exactly with the new holes on the fitting, you'll have to drill new ones which do. Some fittings come without any holes at all because the easiest way to get the holes to align is to drill through the fitting and whatever you're attaching it to at the same time. Then all you have to do is insert the new rivet and "pull" it with a pop rivet tool.

Figure 144 shows the example of replacing a boom end fitting, one of the most likely things you'll have to replace that requires pop riveting. Be sure to insert a foam plug in the boom just past where you'll be drilling a hole for the pop rivet. This will keep the boom from filling up with water when you leave the board tied up to the dock. You can buy these in most board shops. Also be sure to get the boom as far as possible into the fitting. You can check this by measuring the depth of the fitting and marking this depth on the boom prior to

assembly. Then when you hammer and swear the two pieces together, make sure you get up to the mark. Usually four pop rivets per boom fitting will do the trick.

5) Sail repair: The best way to deal with sail repair is through prevention. Take care of your sail! Don't drag it across the rocks. Don't drag it across the dock. Don't tie up your board where someone is likely to run over the sail with their skeg. Always release your downhaul when you store the sail.

Okay, but we all have a bad day once in a while. Suppose you end up with a rip or tear in your sail; whadda ya do? First, stop sailing. Then assess the damage. If it's a small rip or tear, say less than an inch or so long, and not in a particularly high-stress part of the sail or you're sailing only in light winds, chances are you can use it the rest of the day without dire consequences. You're taking your chances, however.

At the very least, small rips and tears should be patched before the next day of use. Often a small patch of "rip stop tape" (available at most sail lofts and boat supply stores) applied to each side of a clean, dry sail will hold up just fine.

If a rip or tear is major enough to cause wrinkles or deformation to appear in the shape of the sail, you should stop sailing

right away. These types of problems will almost always require professional mending so call a local board shop to get a recommendation for a good sail loft. Before you take the sail to the loft, rinse it off and let it dry. After all, you wouldn't take dirty, wet clothes to the tailor, would you?

REPAIRS (TEMPORARY):

Now that we've discussed how to fix your board competently, we should discuss temporary fixes. These are the fixes that you use in order to to be able to keep on sailing the rest of the day. These are not fixes that will hold up!!! While you are making these fixes, you must assure your board that it is only temporary, that you promise a better fix as soon as possible, and that you won't push your board so that the damaged area is highly stressed. With a little luck, maybe your board will cooperate.

These types of fixes shouldn't be used indiscriminately. You are the best judge as to whether or not they should be applied. You must weigh the possibility of doing more damage to your board against your desire to keep sailing.

These types of fixes can be summed up in two words: duct tape. This is the silver looking tape that you can pick up at most hardware stores. You can use it to patch holes and cracks in the board and small rips in the sail as well as hold together cracked fittings or stripped screws. With a little imagination you can really do a lot with this stuff. But remember, it's only temporary!!!

APPENDIX THREE: PERFORMANCE CHARACTERISTICS OF BOARDS

SO YOU'RE REALLY INTO IT AND YOU WANT TO FIND OUT A LITTLE BIT MORE ABOUT WHAT AFFECTS THE PERFORMANCE OF A SAILBOARD. WELL READ ON!

The performance of different types of sailboards varies according to wind and wave conditions and the weight and expertise of the sailor. There are no statements you can make about any particular performance characteristic that cover all conditions and sailors. Following, however, are some general observations that should help you understand the dynamics of sailboard performance as well as how different parts of the sailboard contribute to its overall performance.

VOLUME: The volume of a board affects its weight, its turning characteristics and its flotation. The more volume a board has, the heavier it will be and, in general, additional weight is undesirable. Boards with more volume at the stern will be a bit harder to jibe at high speeds than boards with little volume at the stern. This is because the additional volume prevents you from effectively sinking the rails to carve the turn.

LENGTH: The length of a board will affect both its stability and maneuverability. Longer boards tend to be more stable than shorter boards, both when at rest and when moving. The longer board will also be less maneuverable. The increased wetted surface and weight of the long board will usually make it slower than a short board when reaching. But the increased length and addition of a daggerboard provide greater upwind speed and pointing ability.

WIDTH: Given enough wind, a narrow board will be faster and more stable at high speeds than a wide board. A wide board, given ample flotation, will be much more stable at rest and during maneuvers such as uphauling and tacking. A wide bow will resist nose diving while a wide stern reaches planing speeds more quickly. A narrow stern provides greater maneuverability for carving high speed turns.

ROCKER: Generally speaking, the more rocker a board has, the more maneuverable it will be. Ample nose rocker also lessens your chances of plowing into a wave. Conversely, all other things held equal, boards with less rocker, especially in the stern, are generally faster. Excessive rocker will make a board bog down in the water and slow to start planing.

TAIL SHAPE: Theories abound as to the performance characteristics of different tail shapes. Most of these theories revolve around how much planing area, or wetted surface, at the stern the different tail shapes provide, as well as how easily the different shapes "release" the water flowing past them.

Given enough wind, the tail shapes with less wetted surface at the stern should be faster. This makes sense because when the board is planing on its stern, less wetted surface means less friction between the board and the water. Hence there is less drag and the board is faster.

Likewise, the tail shapes which release water more easily should also be faster. Hydrodynamic testing indicates that sharp corners will release water with greater turbulence but less drag than smooth flowing shapes. For this reason "wings" are often used in conjunction with different tail shapes to enhance hydrodynamic release.

Tail shape will also affect the way a board turns. The pintail, the most widely used tail shape, provides smooth flowing turns while being fairly forgiving. A squash tail is forgiving and achieves planing speeds quickly but is hard to sink during high speed carving turns and is prone to spinning out. The swallow tail has enjoyed only limited popularity.

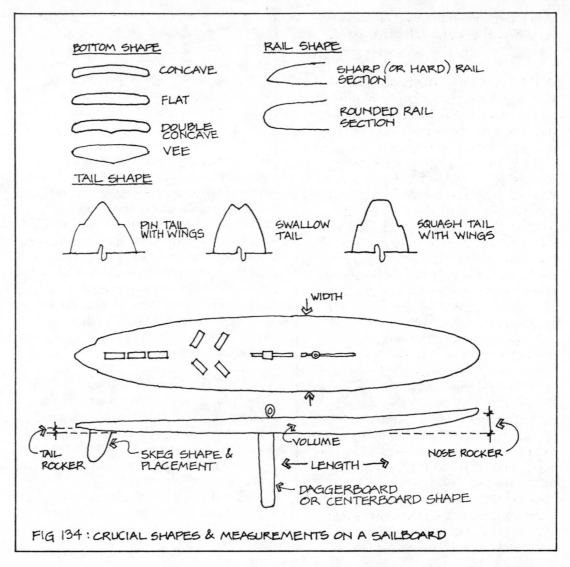

FIG 134: CRUCIAL SHAPES & MEASUREMENTS ON A SAILBOARD

While providing improved performance on surfboards, it doesn't seem to make much of a difference on a sailboard.

BOTTOM SHAPE: The bottom shape of a board will affect its planing ability, speed, maneuverability and stability. On many boards, the bottom shape changes along the length of the board.

A flat bottom is stable and forgiving at rest and at low speeds although it loses much of its stability at high speeds. A double- or multiple-concave board reaches planing speeds very quickly and has good directional stability. If the concavity is deep so that the center of the board is slightly veed, the upwind ability of the board is enhanced. This is often the type of bottom you see on course-racing boards.

High-performance short boards will often have concavity or double concavity at the bow, a flat bottom in the midsections and a flat or veed bottom at the stern. The concavity forward will promote early planing while the flat midsection will promote speed. A veed bottom at the stern will promote maneuverability but is not quite as fast as a flat bottom.

RAIL SHAPE: Hard rails will allow better high speed turning characteristics than rounded rails. For this reason, high-wind boards will almost always have hard

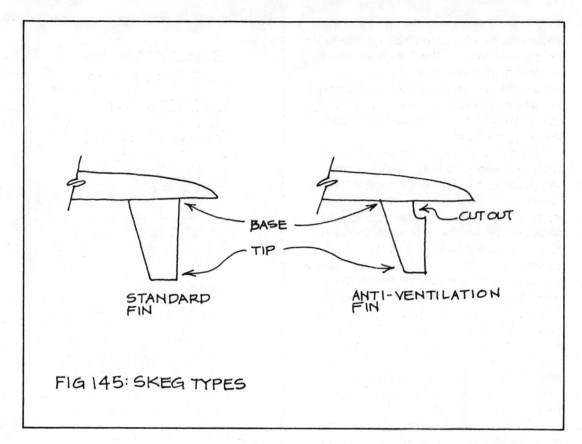

FIG 145: SKEG TYPES

rails at the stern. Hard rails up forward aren't necessary, since most of the forward sections of the board are out of the water when you are planing. Rounded rails at the stern tend to make the board bog down in the water at high speeds and provide mushy, mediocre high-speed turning performance.

FINS (or Skegs): As your board moves through the water, your fin generates hydrodynamic lift which works to counteract and resolve the aerodynamic forces of the sail thus allowing the board to sail forward instead of sideways through the water. As such, a fin provides lateral resistance, upwind ability and directional stability. Additional fin area will provide greater performance in these areas. But additional fin area increases drag and therefore reduces potential speed. Also, excessive fin area at high speeds can cause the fin to develop enough lift to rail the board which, in turn, can lead to a spectacular crash-and-burn, the first step of which is usually a warp-factor-six face plant.

The further aft your fins are mounted, the greater your directional stability will be. Skegs mounted further forward will increase the "looseness" of the board.

Ventilation (often erroneously called cavitation) is connected to fin shape. When the fin ventilates, the result is an

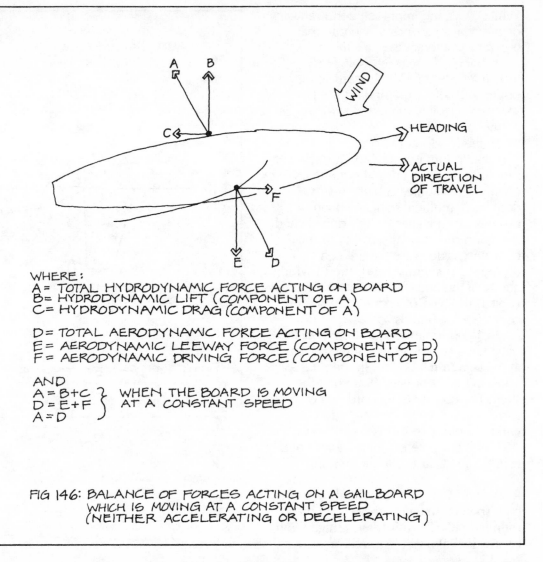

WHERE:
A = TOTAL HYDRODYNAMIC FORCE ACTING ON BOARD
B = HYDRODYNAMIC LIFT (COMPONENT OF A)
C = HYDRODYNAMIC DRAG (COMPONENT OF A)

D = TOTAL AERODYNAMIC FORCE ACTING ON BOARD
E = AERODYNAMIC LEEWAY FORCE (COMPONENT OF D)
F = AERODYNAMIC DRIVING FORCE (COMPONENT OF D)

AND
A = B+C } WHEN THE BOARD IS MOVING
D = E+F } AT A CONSTANT SPEED
A = D }

FIG 146: BALANCE OF FORCES ACTING ON A SAILBOARD WHICH IS MOVING AT A CONSTANT SPEED (NEITHER ACCELERATING OR DECELERATING)

almost total loss of lift and spin-out. Fins with a cut-out (fig. 145) are less prone to ventilation than those without, but also generate lift less efficiently. A fin which is located too far aft can tend to entrain air from the tail of the board thereby being much more susceptible to ventilation and spin out.

DAGGERBOARDS (Centerboards): On a long board your daggerboard will provide a good part of your upwind ability. For maximum upwind performance you want one which provides good lift to windward, low drag and resists stalling.

For the most part, the drag created by a daggerboard will be proportional to its area. The greater the area, the greater the drag. Lift is generated by a daggerboard because when you're pointing, the daggerboard isn't moving symmetrically through the water (fig. 146). The sideways component of the sail's aerodynamic force causes the board to slip a little sideways through the water so that the direction that the board is pointed is not the same as its actual direction of travel. The result of this is that the daggerboard is dragged slightly sideways through the water. As a result there is asymmetrical hydrodynamic flow across the daggerboard creating a low-pressure area on the windward side. This is the same phenomenon responsible for railing

and daggerboard down footsteering. This low-pressure area also works to pull or "lift" the board to windward which, when you're pointing, is the direction you want to go.

Different foil sections provide differing degrees of daggerboard lift. The foil sections which provide maximum lift also operate within a narrow angle of attack and are therefore the most prone to stalling. For maximum performance, it's critical that the daggerboard foil be smooth and fair. Any flat spots or roughness will drastically reduce its effectiveness.

How much effective lift per unit area and therefore per unit drag a daggerboard can generate also depends on the relationship of the length of the daggerboard to its chord depth (fig. 147). A high-aspect daggerboard will generally provide greater lift per unit area but at an increased tendency toward stalling. A low-aspect daggerboard doesn't provide as much lift per unit area but has an increased resistance to stalling.

SAIL SHAPE: A sail's plan, its camber and the stability of its center of effort (CE) all affect its performance. We've already discussed the stable CE issue (pgs. 126-7) so suffice it to say that fully battened sails of mylar or kevlar/mylar combinations make high-wind sailing a lot more

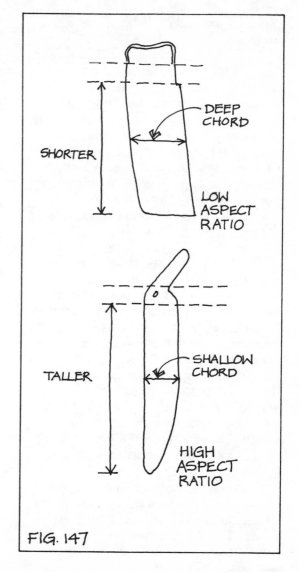

SHORTER

DEEP CHORD

LOW ASPECT RATIO

TALLER

SHALLOW CHORD

HIGH ASPECT RATIO

FIG. 147

pleasant and will probably make you a lot faster.

A sail's plan is its basic outline shape. Like a daggerboard, the efficiency of a sail depends in part on the aspect ratio of its plan. High-aspect sails (short booms and a tall mast) tend to be aerodynamically efficient but prone to stalling and difficult to control due to the height of the CE in the sail. Low-aspect sails tend to be forgiving and easier to control but not tremendously efficient. In either case, a large foot which allows you to "close the gap" (see pg. 78) will dramatically increase the efficiency of the sail.

The camber, or sectional curving profile, of a sail also affects its performance and a lot of research and effort has gone into learning how to control sail camber. When the camber is moved forward (fig 148), there is a greater force vector generated in the forward direction, the direction you want to go! Sails with their camber forward, therefore, are generally faster and more efficient and tend less to cause spin out. Tapered battens, thin end toward the mast, work well to move the camber forward and improve the sail's performance.

Research has also shown that having smooth, attached (as opposed to turbulent, separated) air flow just aft of the leeward side of the mast significantly improves a sail's efficiency and per-

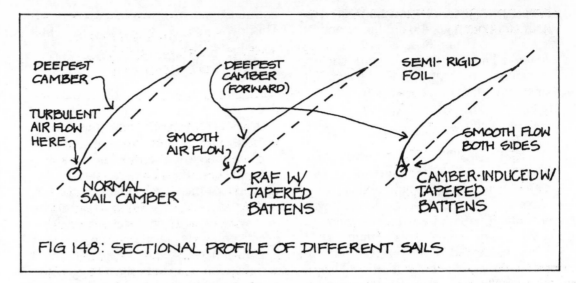

FIG 148: SECTIONAL PROFILE OF DIFFERENT SAILS

formance. For this reason, rotating asymmetrical foil (RAF) sails were developed with a special mast sleeve that allows the battens to rotate to leeward and fill what was often a turbulent pocket on earlier-style sails.

Camber-induced sails combine and enhance the ideas of forward camber and smooth air flow by using special "inducers" which not only increase camber by bending the batten, but also provide smooth air flow around the mast and stabilize the foil shape of the batten. The result is a semi-rigid, high-performance sail.

APPENDIX FOUR: FORWARD AND TO WINDWARD!!!!!

A LITTLE CONFUSED AS TO WHERE "FORWARD & TO WINDWARD" IS? WELL READ ON!

Why is FORWARD AND TO WINDWARD so important? Only because many beginning boardsailors tend to sheet in the sail when it is aft and to leeward, which is, of course, exactly opposite from FORWARD AND TO WINDWARD. It's just a natural tendency! But what that does is cause you to stall out and/or round up, both of which you don't want.

Okay, you want your mast FORWARD AND TO WINDWARD!!! But first a bit of qualification. You don't always want your mast FORWARD AND TO WINDWARD. But in the beginning, you almost always want your board approximately perpendicular to the wind and your mast FORWARD AND TO WINDWARD as you sheet in. One exception to this is when you are sailing in light winds. Then you want your mast a little forward but with the mast leaning neither to windward or to leeward. In very, very light winds you can even tilt your mast forward and little to leeward. This allows gravity to aid in giving the sail a foil shape.

But where is FORWARD AND TO WINDWARD you ask? Okay, imagine seeing your sailboard in side view (fig. 149). Now imagine a dotted line drawn straight up from the mast foot. Anything in front of that line is FORWARD. Okay?

Now imagine a back view of your board with the same line drawn (fig. 150). Anything toward the direction of the wind is TO WINDWARD. Okay?

Now let's look at the board from the top (fig. 151) drawing a dotted line the length of the board to separate windward from leeward and another line across the board to separate forward from aft. By doing this, we've successfully divided the diagram into four quadrants one of which is where FORWARD coincides with TO WINDWARD. This quadrant is, therefore, FORWARD AND TO WINDWARD. Okay?

When you're first learning to windsurf, unless the wind is very light, you'll want to sheet in with the mast in the FORWARD AND TO WINDWARD quadrant. If you have the mast in the forward and to leeward quadrant as you sheet in, you'll either stall the board or steer radically downwind. If you have the mast in either of the aft quadrants as you sheet in, you'll round up. FORWARD AND TO WINDWARD!!! Okay?

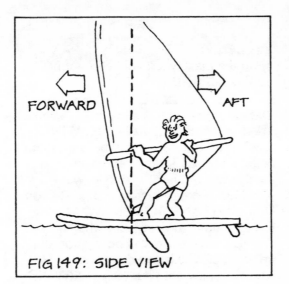

FIG 149: SIDE VIEW

FIG 150: BACK VIEW

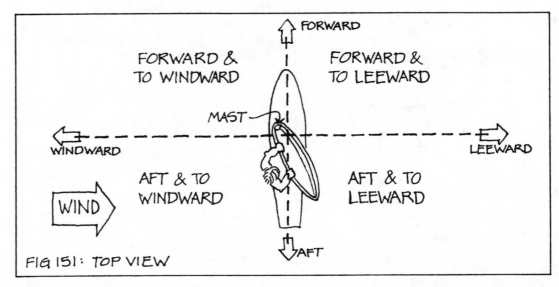

FIG 151: TOP VIEW

Zen and the Art of Windsurfing

A SHORT DICTIONARY OF WINDSURFING TERMS:

A

Aft, adj.; Toward or behind the stern of the board.

After Hand, n.; The hand furthest away from the mast when you are in normal sailing position. See also Boom Hand and Back Hand.

Aggg!!, interj.; Colloquial phrase used to indicate dismay, displeasure or impending doom.

Apparent Wind, n.; The speed and direction of the wind as it appears to a body (yours) not at rest.

Arggg!!, interj.; Variation of Aggg. See above.

Aspect Ratio, n.; Ratio between the height of the mast and the length of the boom or the height and length of a daggerboard.

Asymmetrical Board, n.; Specialty board used for sailing waves that characteristically break in a certain direction.

B

Back Hand, n.; The hand furthest away from the mast when you're in normal sailing position.

Batten, n.; Slender, stiff piece of material used to stiffen the roach of the sail.

Bear Away, v.; To steer to leeward.

Bear Off, v.; To bear away.

Beat, v.; 1.To sail to windward. See also Point. 2.What you want to do to your rivals in a race. —adj.; How you feel after you've done what you want to do to your rivals in a race.

Beaufort's Scale, n.; Scale used to measure wind speed with Forces instead of MPH or Knots. Force 0 equals calm, force 5 equals 20 knots and force 10 equals 50 knots.

Blank, n.; Solid block of foam from which a custom board is shaped. —adj.; expression worn by a windsurfer waiting for wind.

Boom, n.; Part of the rig that holds the clew of the sail.

Boom Hand, n.; Same as Back Hand.

Booties, n. pl.; Black rubber shoes you wear to keep your feet warm.

Bow, n.; Sailor talk for front end.

Bungee Cord, n.; Elasticized rope used for, among other things, bungeed uphauls.

By the lee, adv.; Sailing such that, when the sail is properly trimmed, the clew is further to windward than the luff. Reserved for jibing, freestyle tricks and embarrassing accidents.

C

Camber, n.; Sectional curvature of the sail.

Carve, v.; To steer with foot pressure (she just ~ed a great jibe).

Catapult, n.; 1.High-wind method of leaving the sailboard. 2.Something injurious to one's psyche. —v.; The act of performing a catapult.

Cautiously, adj.; How you proceed after a catapult.

Cavitation, n.; The result of entraining air at the skeg(s). Causes you to spin out. More precisely called ventilation (see pg. 144)

Centerboard, n.; Large foil-shaped blade used to increase lateral resistance and improve upwind performance of larger sailboards. It can be pivoted back and withdrawn into the board.

Center of Effort (CE), n.; Imaginary focal point of the aerodynamic forces acting upon the sail.

Center of Lateral Resistance (CLR), n.; Imaginary focal point of the forces in a sailboard that resist lateral movement.

Clew, n.; One of the corners of the sail.

Close-Hauled,adv.; To sail as far to windward as possible, to be pointing.

Come Up, v.; To steer further to windward.

Crash-and-Burn, n.; A maneuver enjoyed by everyone but the person who does it.

Custom, n.; One-of-a-kind sailboard made to the buyer's specifications.

D

Dacron, n.; A type of sail cloth.

Daggerboard, n.; Large foil-shaped blade used to increase the lateral resistance and upwind performance of larger sailboards. It differs from a centerboard in that it cannot be retracted into the board but must be manually withdrawn.

Daggerboard Slot (or well), n.; Where one puts one's daggerboard if one is fairly conventional about one's approach to one's sailboard.

Double Concave, adj.; High-performance bottom shape for sailboards.

Down, adj.; To leeward.

Downhaul, n.; Line used to tension the luff of the sail. Attaches to the tack.

Downwind, adj.; To leeward, away from the direction of the wind.

Draft, adj.; Term used to describe the depth or fullness of a sail.

Drysuit, n.; Like a wetsuit but designed to keep the water out. Very warm.

Duck Jibe, n.; An advanced type of jibe where the sailor ducks beneath the sail during the jibe instead of letting the boom swing over the bow.

Duck Tack, n.; A special kind of tack where the sailor ducks under the boom instead of walking around the mast. Not used very much.

Duct Tape, n.; That silver-looking tape used to repair just about anything.

E

Epoxy, n.; Special type of high-strength resin used in making and repairing boards and masts.

F

Fall off, v.; 1.To steer to leeward, to bear away. 2.To involuntarily relinquish one's position on the sailboard.

Fast, adj.; Word used to describe sailboards in general.

Fin, n.; Another name for Skeg.

Fin Box, n.; The slotted box into which you fasten your fin.

Floater, n.; A sailboard that can support a sailor and rig while at rest thereby allowing the sailor to uphaul.

Flotation, n.; Amount of buoyancy a board has.

Foot, n.; The part of your sail below your boom.

Footsteer, v.; To use your feet to tilt the board in order to steer it.

Footstrap, n.; 1.Hoop of material screwed to the deck of the board into which you stick your foot. More convenient and comfortable than your mouth.

Forward, adj.; Toward or in front of the bow of the board.

Forward Hand, n.; Hand nearest the mast when in normal sailing position.

Freestyle, n.; Sailboard gymnastics.

Front Hand, n.; Not the back hand. See Forward Hand.

Fully Battened, adj.; A type of sail with battens running all the way from the mast to the leech.

Funboard, n.; Name for general use, high-wind sailboard.

G

Gun, n.; Moderate length board, very narrow at the stern and built for all-out speed.

Gust, n.; Sudden increase in wind speed.

H

Hard Rails, n. pl.; Denotes sharpness in the rail section of the board.

Harden Up, v.; To steer to windward. See Come Up.

Harness, n.; Contraption you wear which attaches you to the boom, sometimes when least expected or desired.

Harness Line, n.; What you hook your harness to.

Head, n.; Top of the sail.

Head Off, v.; To bear away or steer to leeward.

Header, n.; A change in wind direction to leeward.

Hydroplane, v.; 1.To skip across the surface of the water. 2.The whole point of windsurfing.

Hypothermia, n.; A serious lowering of body temperature caused by exposure and which, in extreme cases, can result in death.

I

Induced wind, n.; The wind observed by a moving body (yours) caused by the movement of that body.

Inhaul, n.; The thing that holds the mast to the boom.

J

Jibe, v.; To turn such that the board's stern passes through the direction of the oncoming wind. —n.; The product of jibing.

Jive, v.; To lie or exaggerate esp. while telling sailing stories. —n.; The product of jiving (what's that ∼ meatball?)

K

Knot, n.; 1.Like a MPH only bigger, used to measure wind speed. 2.Something that will never come untied when you want it to. 3.That feeling you get in the pit of your stomach when you first notice that freighter behind you.

L

Leech, n.; Aft edge of the sail.

Leeward, adj.; Direction away from the direction of the oncoming wind. Not to windward.

Lift, n.; Change in wind direction to windward. Opposite of Header.

Loft, n.; Place where sails are designed, built and repaired.

Long John, n.; Type of sleeveless wetsuit usually worn with a jacket.

Luff, n.; Part of the sail nearest to the mast.

Lull, n.; Sudden decrease in wind speed.

M

Mast, n.; The long skinny thing.

Mast Foot, n.; What goes at the end of the mast enabling you to attach it to the board.

Mast Foot Well, n.; Another name for mast step.

Mast Sleeve, n.; Part of the sail into which you slip the mast.

Mast Step, n.; Part of the board where the mast foot attaches.

Mast Tether, n.; A small line which attaches the rig to the board in case of rig separation during a bad fall.

Mast Track, n.; Device which allows the mast step to be moved fore and aft while sailing.

Mylar, n.; Type of sail cloth.

O

Offshore, adj.; Away from the shore (an ~ wind).

Off the Wind, adj.; To be sailing on a reach or run, not pointing.

Onshore, adj.; Toward the shore (an ~ wind).

On the Wind, adj.; To point or sail to windward.

One Design, n.; 1.A mass-produced board. 2.Identical boards which race together (a ~ fleet).

One Off, n.; A custom board.

Outhaul, n.; Device for tensioning the sail at the clew.

Overpowered, adj.; The state that results when you have too much sail area for the conditions. Marked by frustration and fear. Generally undesired.

P

PFD, n. abbr.; (personal flotation device) life jacket, required (by law) in some states.

Pinch, v.; To sail so far to windward that the sail depowers and the board begins to stall.

Plane, v.; 1.Short for to hydroplane. 2.The whole point of windsurfing.

Point, v.; To sail as high on the wind as possible.

Polyester, n.; Type of resin used to make some boards.

Port, adj.; 1.Left-hand side. 2.Not starboard.

Power Joint, n.; The pivoting or turning joint between the mast foot and the board.

Production Board, n.; A mass-produced board.

Pump, v.; Rapid trimming or flapping of the sail which causes the board to move through the water. Hopefully, at a higher rate of speed.

Purl (also Pearl), v.; 1.The action of (accidently) sinking the bow of your board while sailing. 2.Action immediately preceding a crash-and-burn. 3.Action immediately preceding the use of Arggg! (see above).

Puff, n; 1.Another name for a gust. 2.The name of the dog that belonged to the fat lady that lived across the street in the neighborhood where you grew up.

R

Radical, adj.; 1.A term used to describe an unusual crash-and-burn. 2.(semi-archaic) Term used to describe a short, high-wind board 3.(extremely archaic) Abbey Hoffman.

RAF (Rotating Asymmetrical Foil), n.; A special type of fully battened sail which allows the battens to rotate around the mast thereby increasing the efficiency of the sail shape.

Rail, v.; When the board turns up on its edge due to asymmetrical flow over the daggerboard or fin. —n.; The length-wise edge of the board.

Reach, v.; To sail nearly perpendicular to the wind. Point(s) of sail between point-ing and running.

Rig, n.; The unit of the sail, mast, boom and mast foot all together.

Right of Way, n.; 1.The legal, moral or ethical justification for denying culpability in the case of a collision. 2.Something discussed in front of a race committee or in a court of law. 3.Something vaguely understood.

Roach, n.; 1.The part of the sail beyond a straight line drawn from the clew to the head.

Rocker, n.; Measurement of curvature of the hull.

Round Up, v.; 1.When the board steers suddenly and dramatically to windward against your will. —n.;1.Action just prior to a slam dunk. 2.Action associated with the intensive use of slang.

Run, v.; To sail downwind. —n. A downwind leg or course.

S

Sailboard, n.; A small, fast, exciting, inexpensive sailboat. —v.; To windsurf.

Sailboat, n.; 1.A large, slow sailboard. 2.Object owned by the bank but lent to you in return for huge monthly pay-ments. 3.Metaphysical object of desire among those unfamiliar with the reality of owning one.

Scoop, n.; Another name for rocker.

Sharp Rails, n. pl.; Another name for hard rails.

Simulator, n.; 1.A sailboard without skeg or daggerboard used to practice on dry land. 2.A contraption specifically built for this purpose.

Skeg, n.; A foil-shaped fin at the stern of the board which provides lateral resistance and directional stability.

Skeg Ventilation, v.; The entrainment of air by the skeg causing it to lose its bite. The result is spin out.

Slam Dunk, n.; A favorite maneuver of beginning windsurfers. Caused by rounding up.

Spin Out, v.; To spin to windward as a result of skeg ventilation

Spreader Bar, n.; Bar used with a harness to alleviate inward pressure on the rib cage.

Stall, v.; To interrupt the hydrodynamic movement of the board or aerodynamic movement of the sail so that flow becomes turbulent and sideways motion is induced.

Steer Down, v.; To steer to leeward.

Steer Up, v.; To steer to windward.

T

Tack, v.; To turn such that the bow of the board passes through the direction of the oncoming wind. —n. The corner of the sail where you attach the downhaul.

Tell Tale, n.; Streamer attached to the sail to help determine where the wind is coming from and whether or not the sail is properly trimmed.

Thruster, n.; Small skeg usually used in pairs in conjunction with a large skeg on short boards.

Transition Board, n.; Medium length, medium buoyancy board used to make the learning transition from long to short boards

Trim, v.; To adjust the sail for optimum performance.

True Wind, n.; The direction and speed of the wind as measured from a stationary observation point.

U

Uggg!, interj.; Statement of dismay and disgust. Often used when forced ashore in the vicinity of mud flats and salt-water marshes.

Universal, n.; The flexible joint between the mast and the board.

Up, adj.; To windward.

Uphaul, n.; The thing you use to pull the sail out of the water. —v.; To pull the sail out of the water.

Upwind, adj,; To windward.

V

Ventilation n.; Act of entraining air at the skeg(s). Causes spin-out. Often erroneously called cavitation.

Volume, n.; The measure of the buoyancy of a sailboard.

W

Water Start, n.; Maneuver in which you let the wind pull you and the sail up and out of the water.

Wax, n.; Stuff you rub on your board to keep your feet from slipping.

Weather, adj.; To windward (the first leg of the race was to ~)

Wetted Surface, n.; Area of the bottom of the board which comes in contact with the water.

Window, n.; Clear part of the sail.

Windsurfer, n.; 1.You. 2.Others like you. 3.Another name for sailboarder or board-sailor. 4.The brand name of the sailboard that started it all.

Windward, adj.; Toward the direction of the oncoming wind.

Wings, n.,pl.; Small steps in the rails near the stern which theoretically reduce drag.

Y

Yikes, interj.; Expression of surprise.

Yipes, interj.; Variation of Yikes, see above.

Z

Zen, n., A philosophically based religious doctrine that can be used to soothe and pacify in periods of severe physical and psychological stress; which, at times, can be productively employed when you're first learning to windsurf.

INDEX

ABOUT THE AUTHOR:

Frank Fox is an architect-turned-author who loves boardsailing. Frank just bought a new course board and four new sails on his credit card. Therefore, he wishes to thank you for buying this book, thereby contributing a small increment to the reduction of his debt. He also hopes that you will buy his newest boardsailing book *Windsurfing 1. to boardsail* for which we've put an order form in the back of this book.

Frank welcomes comments and criticisms on this book which can be sent to him in care of the publisher.

ABOUT THE TECHNICAL ASSISTANTS

Catherine "Cat" Betts, a resident of the San Francisco Bay Area, is a former professional speed skier who is now a professional boardsailor. She has written for national boardsailing magazines and is currently on FANATIC's United States sailboard racing team where she is compiling an impressive record of victories.

With over twenty-five years experience sailing on San Francisco Bay, Bard Chrisman's nautical endeavors include dinghy and displacement boat racing and sailing, custom boat building and carpentry, spar building and nautical equipment fabrication. He is truly a well-rounded expert sailor.

An avid boardsailor since the sport emerged in the early 1970's, Bard has pioneered advances in sailboarding technology through the design and fabrication of custom boards and sailboard equipment. Bard shapes custom boards and anyone interested in having a board shaped can contact him by writing to Bard Chrisman, 1219 Central B, Alameda, CA 94501.

THE AMAZING, WORLD FAMOUS ZACHARY DOOLITTLE ORDER FORM

Dear Zach,

I read your book and I thought it was (circle one) A) Great B) Okay C) Terrible D) Confusing. My only suggestion would be to A) Make it shorter B) Rewrite it C) Translate it into Japanese D) Sell it to the Russians as a military secret. Anyhow, I need more copies because A) The one I had was borrowed B) I left mine at the beach C) My guests are bored with the magazines I have in the bathroom D) My dog mistook my original copy for a bone.

Also, I hear your creator has another book out called *Windsurfing 1. to boardsail*, a dictionary of amusing boardsailing definitions. Please send me some copies of that since A) I'd like to give it to my Aunt Hilda for her eighty-first birthday B) We're out of old newpapers to start fires with C) My therapist recommends it D) I'm going to sell it to the Russians as a military secret.

So enclosed you'll find a check or money order for $8.95 for each book like this one that I want and $6.95 for each dictionary that I want plus $1.50 per order to cover shipping* and handling. I'll make the check or money order out to Amberco Press and send it to you C/O AMBERCO, P.O. Box 5038, Berkeley, CA 94705.

Sincerely,

(name)_____

(address)_____

(city, state)_____

(zip)_____

(# Zen books x $8.95)_____

(# dictionaries x $6.95)_____

(Shipping)_____$1.50_____

(Tax**)_____

(Total)_____

* We usually ship via UPS which doesn't deliver to P.O. boxes. If your address is a P.O. box, we'll ship your order book rate or include an extra $2.00 for first-class mail.

** California residents only, 54 cents per Zen book, 42 cents per dictionary.